INSECT KINGDOM

John Farndon and Dr Jen Green

Consultants
Michael Chinery and Mathew Frith

southwater

This edition is published by Southwater

Southwater is an imprint of Anness Publishing Ltd
Hermes House, 88–89 Blackfriars Road, London SE1 8HA
tel. 020 7401 2077; fax 020 7633 9499
www.southwaterbooks.com; info@anness.com

© Anness Publishing Ltd 2004

UK agent: The Manning Partnership Ltd, 6 The Old Dairy,
Melcombe Road, Bath BA2 3LR; tel. 01225 478444; fax 01225 478440;
sales@manning-partnership.co.uk

UK distributor: Grantham Book Services Ltd, Isaac Newton Way,
Alma Park Industrial Estate, Grantham, Lincs NG31 9SD;
tel. 01476 541080; fax 01476 541061; orders@gbs.tbs-ltd.co.uk

North American agent/distributor: National Book Network,
4501 Forbes Boulevard, Suite 200, Lanham, MD 20706;
tel. 301 459 3366; fax 301 429 5746; www.nbnbooks.com

Australian agent/distributor: Pan Macmillan Australia,
Level 18, St Martins Tower, 31 Market St, Sydney, NSW 2000;
tel. 1300 135 113; fax 1300 135 103; customer.service@macmillan.com.au

New Zealand agent/distributor: David Bateman Ltd, 30 Tarndale Grove,
Off Bush Road, Albany, Auckland; tel. (09) 415 7664; fax (09) 415 8892

All rights reserved. No part of this publication may be reproduced, stored
in a retrieval system, or transmitted in any way or by any means,
electronic, mechanical, photocopying, recording or otherwise, without
the prior written permission of the copyright holder.

A CIP catalogue record for this book is available from the British Library.

10 9 8 7 6 5 4 3 2 1

Publisher: Joanna Lorenz
Project Editors: Rebecca Clunes,
Nicole Pearson, Dawn Titmus,
Sarah Uttridge and
Elizabeth Woodland
Copy Editors: Simon Beecroft,
Nicky Barber and Sarah Eason
Designers: Vivienne Gordon and Jill Mumford
Jacket Design: Alix Wood
Illustrators: Julian Baker, Vanessa Card, Stuart Carter,
Rob Sheffield and David Webb
Special Photography: Kim Taylor
Picture Researchers: Su Alexander and Liz Heasman
Prepress Controller: Neil McLaren
Production Controller: Darren Price

Previously published in two separate volumes,
Nature Watch: Beetles and Bugs and *Nature
Watch: Butterflies and Moths*

CONTENTS

INTRODUCTION

Of all the creatures on the Earth, insects are the among the tiniest. There are over a million known species of insect, and thousands of new species are discovered every year. Insects live almost everywhere, from steamy tropical jungles to icy polar regions. There are insects living inside houses and at the summit of the highest mountains, in caves deep underground and in the branches of tall trees. They live everywhere except the oceans.

▲ CARPET BEETLE GRUB
Many beetles are regarded as pests, like this carpet beetle grub, which can chew its way through woolen carpets and clothes. Adult carpet beetles are harmless and feed on flowers.

Beetles and butterflies could hardly look more different. Beetles are the tanks of the insect world. They have tough, compact, armor plated bodies, move about mostly by crawling, and many live in the ground. Butterflies, by contrast, are beautiful, delicate creatures, with their huge colorful wings. They are agile and often able to fly vast distances. However, beetles and butterflies have more in common than you might think. Like all insects, they have bodies divided into three sections (head, abdomen and thorax), six legs and antennae on the head. They both also have two pairs of wings as adults. You may not realize that beetles have wings, because they do not use them that often, but the hard shell on the beetle's body is not actually a shell, but its tough front wings, which fold closed over its back wings.

Some beetles are so small you can see them only with a magnifying glass. The hairy-winged dwarf beetle is just ⅟₆₄th inch long. The African dwarf blue butterfly is barely ½ inch across, and most of that is wing. However, there are beetles and butterflies that are among the largest of all insects. Acteon beetles from Central America are one of the bulkiest and heaviest of all insects, more than 5 inches long and 4 inches wide. African Goliath beetles are as big, while no insect has wings larger than the owlet moth of tropical America, whose wingspan is 18 inches.

▲ BIG BEETLE
The Goliath beetles of western Africa are among the world's biggest, bulkiest insects—and it is not just the adults that are big. Their grubs are like big sausages up to 6 inches long and weighing as much as a baking potato.

With over 350,000 different kinds of beetle, and 55,000 kinds of bug and over 165,000 kinds of butterfly and moth, it is hard to imagine just how many individual beetles and bugs there are. A survey in Pennsylvania showed that there were 25 million grubs (the young) of just one kind of beetle, the click beetle, living in every acre of soil—and the click beetle is just one of 23,700 known kinds of beetle in the U.S.A. Scientists estimate that there are 10 quintillion insects alive at any one time (that is 10 followed by 18 noughts)—and a huge proportion of these are beetles, bugs, butterflies and moths.

▼ **APOLLO BUTTERFLY**

The beautiful Apollo butterfly lives on high mountains and is well adapted to the cold. But many Apollo populations have come under threat from polluted air and the growth in tourism. One subspecies in Poland has been reduced to just 20 butterflies.

All these insects play a crucial role in maintaining our environment. Many plants could not grow and spread without butterflies and moths to carry their pollen from flower to flower. Beetles help turn over the soil and break down rotting vegetable and animal matter—especially in forests, which would soon become choked with dead plants and trees without them. Beetles also help to keep down numbers of pest species, such as caterpillars. Gardeners love ladybug beetles because they feed on the aphids that can wreak havoc with their best plants. Of course, there are a few beetles whose effects on our crops, garden plants and homes is anything but beneficial—cotton boll weevils destroy cotton crops, rootworms attack food stores and carpet beetles eat carpets.

Unfortunately, many butterflies and beetles are facing extinction because their living spaces are being destroyed, their food plants are being uprooted, and because of farming insecticides. There are 27 species of American butterfly and moth that are now endangered, and the Xerces blue butterfly is completely extinct. Many beetle species are threatened, too, including the California Valley Elderberry Longhorn beetle. Some butterflies and beetles are now so rare that they fetch huge prices among insect collectors. Only by learning and understanding more about beetles and butterflies can we hope to ensure their survival which may be more important to our own future than we can imagine.

◄ **DUNG ROLLER**

Dung beetles are fondly regarded by cattle farmers. Cows will not feed on pasture covered in manure, so the dung beetles do farmers a great favor by clearing away most cow manure in just a few days.

BEETLES AND BUGS

Many insects have long, thin bodies and delicate wings, but beetles and bugs both have broad, bulky bodies. Although most can fly, they tend to spend much of the time crawling around. Some people call all insects bugs, but for scientists bugs are a particular group of broad-bodied insects, including bedbugs, assassin bugs and cicadas. Beetles are the largest order of animals on the planet, making up almost a quarter of all the world's animal species.

Nature's Success Story

If you were an alien visiting Earth, which creature would you consider the main life form? We humans like to think we dominate Earth, but insects are far more successful. There are over one million different species (kinds) of insects, compared to just one human species.

Scientists divide insects into groups called orders. The insects in each order share certain features. Beetles and bugs are two major insect orders. The main difference between them is that beetles have biting jaws and bugs have sucking mouthparts. Beetles are the largest order of all. So far, 350,000 different kinds of beetles and 55,000 different kinds of bugs have been found.

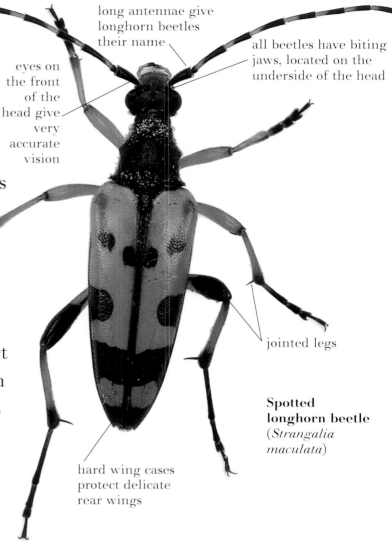

long antennae give longhorn beetles their name

all beetles have biting jaws, located on the underside of the head

eyes on the front of the head give very accurate vision

jointed legs

Spotted longhorn beetle (*Strangalia maculata*)

hard wing cases protect delicate rear wings

▲ THE BEETLE ORDER

Beetles belong to the order Coleoptera, which means "sheath wings." Most beetles have two pairs of wings. The tough front wings fold over the delicate rear wings to form a hard, protective sheath, like body armor. Longhorn beetles owe their name to their long antennae (feelers), which look like long horns.

◄ LIVING IN WATER

Not all beetles and bugs live on land. Some, like this diving beetle (*Dytiscus marginalis*), live in fresh water. The diving beetle hunts under water, diving down to look for food on the stream bed.

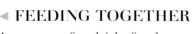

◀ **FEEDING TOGETHER**

A group of aphids feeds on a plant stem, sucking up liquid sap. Most beetles and bugs live alone, but a few species, such as aphids, gather together in large numbers. Although they do not form a community, as ants and bees do, living in a group does give some protection from predators.

What's in a Name?
This image comes from the animated feature film A Bug's Life. *The hero of the cartoon is not actually a bug at all, but an ant. True bugs are a particular group of insects with sucking mouthparts that can slurp up liquid food.*

Forest shield bug
(*Pentatoma rufipes*)

six legs keep the bug stable as it scurries along the ground

◀ **THE BUG ORDER**

Bugs come in many shapes and sizes. All have long, jointed mouthparts that form a tube through which they suck up liquid food, like a syringe. Their order name is Hemiptera, which means "half wings." The name refers to the front wings of many bugs, such as shield bugs, which are hard at the base and flimsy at the tip. With their wings closed, shield bugs are shaped like a warrior's shield.

Did you know? *Insects are unique in having six legs – three on either side.*

THE YOUNG ONES ▶

Young beetles, called grubs or larvae, look very different from adult beetles. A young cockchafer (*Melolontha melolontha*) feeds on plant roots in the soil. Almost all young beetles and bugs hatch from eggs. They pass through several stages in their life cycle.

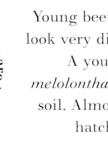

All Kinds of Beetles

One in every five animals on Earth is a beetle. These insects owe much of their success to their natural body armor, which protects them against attack. Beetles are found all over the world, except in Antarctica and in the oceans. Long-nosed weevils, ground beetles, ladybugs, scarabs and glowing fireflies are all major beetle groups.

Goliath beetle
(Goliathus goliatus)

◄▲ LARGEST AND SMALLEST
Beetles come in various sizes. Goliath beetles from Africa (left) are one of the largest beetles, and one of the largest insects of all. They grow up to 6 inches in length and weigh up to ¼ pound. At the other end of the scale, feather-winged beetles are tiny—under ¹⁄₁₆th inch long and smaller than a pinhead. Hairy-winged dwarf beetles are only ¹⁄₆₄th inch long. The tiny beetles (above) are foraging in a flower.

Hercules beetle
(Dynastes hercules)

SCARY SIGHT ►
Hercules beetles are named after the classical hero Hercules, who was famous for his strength. The tough, curved cuticle on the male's head forms huge horns, which he uses to fight and frighten away other males.

Desert scarab
(Scarabaeidae)

Weevil
(Curculionidae)

▲ **BRIGHT AND BEAUTIFUL**

This beetle is a desert scarab from the western United States. There are more than 20,000 species in the scarab family alone. Most are brown, black, green or red, but some are gold, blue, rainbow-colored or white. Scarab beetles are an important part of the food chain because they eat dung, returning its nutrients to the soil.

▲ **LONG-NOSED WEEVILS**

Weevils are the largest family of beetles. There are over 40,000 species. They are also called snout beetles, because of their long noses that scientists call rostrums. The beetle's jaws, and sometimes its eyes, are found at the tip of the long snout. The antennae are often positioned halfway down the beetle's rostrum.

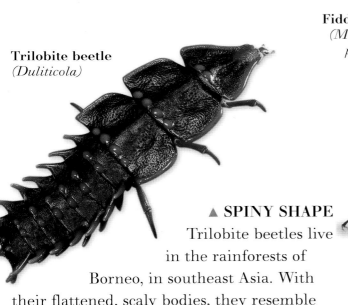

Trilobite beetle
(*Duliticola*)

Fiddle beetle
(*Mormolycei phyllodes*)

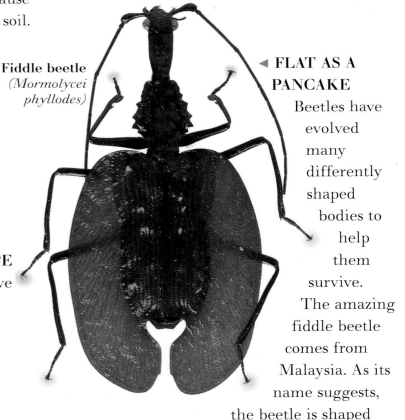

◀ **FLAT AS A PANCAKE**

Beetles have evolved many differently shaped bodies to help them survive. The amazing fiddle beetle comes from Malaysia. As its name suggests, the beetle is shaped like a violin. Fiddle beetles are almost flat, which helps them slip between the flat bracket fungi on the trees in which they live.

▲ **SPINY SHAPE**

Trilobite beetles live in the rainforests of Borneo, in southeast Asia. With their flattened, scaly bodies, they resemble trilobites, a group of armored sea creatures that died out millions of years ago. Unlike most insects, trilobite beetles do not have wings and cannot fly away to escape their enemies. However, the sharp spines on their bodies keep most predators at bay.

11

Bugs of Every Kind

Like beetles, bugs live on every continent except Antarctica. They are found both on dry land and in fresh water. They are so small that they are rarely noticed by people and can survive on very little food. All bugs have piercing and sucking mouthparts, which are tucked beneath their heads when not in use. Many bugs suck juicy sap from plants. Some hunt other insects and suck their juices instead.

Bugs are made up of two large groups. True bugs form one group, whose scientific name is Heteroptera, meaning "different wings." Their front wings have hard bases and thin tips. True bugs include waterscorpions, assassin bugs, shield bugs and bedbugs. Other bugs belong to the group Homoptera, which means "same wings." These bugs have one or two pairs of wings that are the same texture all over. They include leafhoppers, aphids, scale insects and cicadas.

Cicada
(Cicadidae)

▲ BIGGEST AND SMALLEST
Cicadas are one of the largest bugs, growing up to 2 inches long with a wingspan of up to 6 inches. Giant water bugs, also called "toe-biters," grow up to 5 inches long. The whitefly is one of the smallest bugs—at only ⅟₁₆th inch long, it is almost too tiny to be seen by the naked human eye.

STRANGE BUGS ▶
Like beetles, bugs vary a lot in shape. Scale insects owe their name to the hard scale that covers and protects the body of the females. Scale insects are unusual bugs. Most adult females have no legs, wings or antennae, and don't look like insects at all! The males have wings but no scale and look rather like tiny midges.

Scale insects
(Coccoidae)

Shield bug
(*Palomena prasina*)

▲ CROSSED WINGS
Shield bugs have broad, flattened bodies. This species is dull in color, but some are bright scarlet, blue or green. When resting, the shield bug crosses its front wings over its back so that its wing tips overlap. From above, the wings form an X-shape by which you can identify true bugs—the Heteroptera group.

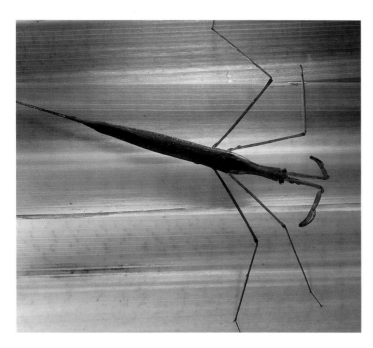

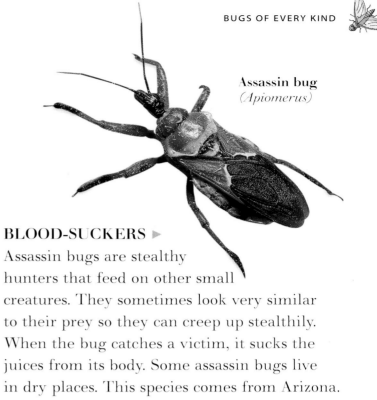

Assassin bug
(*Apiomerus*)

BLOOD-SUCKERS ▶

Assassin bugs are stealthy hunters that feed on other small creatures. They sometimes look very similar to their prey so they can creep up stealthily. When the bug catches a victim, it sucks the juices from its body. Some assassin bugs live in dry places. This species comes from Arizona.

▲ **WATER LOVERS**

Waterscorpions (*Ranatra linearis*) live in ponds and streams. They have long, slender legs and bodies, which camouflage them from enemies. On the insect's rear is a long, thin spine, which it uses as a breathing tube. The bug draws in air from above the surface, while the rest of its body remains submerged.

Useful Bugs

Some types of bugs, including scale insects, are used by people. The bodies of cochineal scales can be crushed to extract cochineal, a red dye. The Aztecs of Mexico used cochineal dye hundreds of years ago.

▲ **LIVING LANTERN**

The lantern bug (*Fulgora*) is named for the pale tip on its snout. Although it looks like a tiny lantern, the tip does not give out light. This bug lives in the rainforests of southeast Asia. Another type of lantern bug has a huge false head, which looks like an alligator's snout.

Body Parts

Garden chafer
(*Phyllopertha horticola*)

head
thorax
abdomen

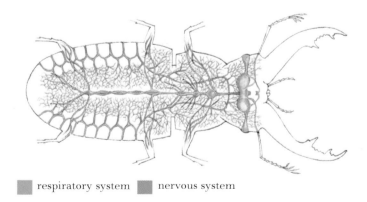

Human bodies are supported by a bony skeleton. Beetles, bugs and other insects have no inner skeleton. Instead, they are protected by a hard outer layer called an exoskeleton. This layer is waterproof and also helps to prevent the insect from drying out in hot weather. The exoskeleton is airtight, but it has special holes called spiracles that allow the insect to breathe.

The word "insect" comes from a Latin word meaning "in sections." Like other insects, beetles' and bugs' bodies are made up of three main parts. All have a head, a thorax (middle section) and an abdomen (rear section). Almost all adult beetles and bugs have six legs, and most have two pairs of wings, which enable them to fly.

▲ THREE SECTIONS

A beetle's main sense organs, the antennae and eyes, are on its head. Its wings and legs are attached to the thorax. The abdomen contains the digestive and reproductive organs. When on the ground, the abdomen is covered by the beetle's wings.

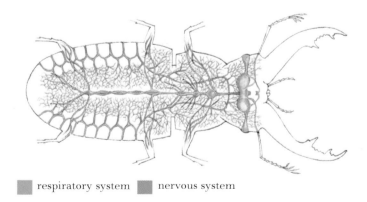

respiratory system nervous system

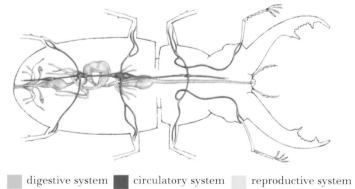

digestive system circulatory system reproductive system

▲ BREATHING AND NERVOUS SYSTEMS

The respiratory (breathing) system has spiracles (openings) that lead to a network of tubes. The tubes allow air to reach all parts of the insect's body. The nervous system receives messages from the sense organs, and sends signals to the insect's muscles to make it move.

▲ OTHER BODY SYSTEMS

The digestive system breaks down and absorbs food. The circulatory system includes a long, thin heart that pumps blood through the body. The abdomen contains the reproductive parts. Males have two testes that produce sperm. Females have two ovaries that produce eggs.

◄ IN COLD BLOOD

Like all insects, beetles and bugs are cold-blooded animals. This means that the temperature of their body is similar to their surroundings. Insects control their body temperature by moving about. To warm up, beetles and bugs bask in the sun, as this leaf beetle (Chrysomelidae) is doing. If they need to cool their bodies, they move into the shade.

SURVIVING THE COLD ►

This tiger beetle egg (*Cicindela*) is buried in the soil. In some parts of the world, winters are too cold for most adult insects to survive. The adult insects die, but their eggs, or young, can survive in the soil because it is warmer. When spring arrives, the young insects emerge, and so the species survives.

Rhinoceros beetle
(Megasoma elephas)

BEETLE CAR

During the 1940s, the tough, rounded beetle shape inspired the German car manufacturer Volkswagen to produce one of the world's most popular family cars, the VW Beetle. The car's tough outer shell, just like that of a beetle, helped it to achieve a good safety record. The design proved so successful that the Beetle car was recently improved and relaunched.

▲ MOVING FORTRESS

The rhinoceros beetle is very well armored. Its tough exoskeleton covers and protects its whole body. The cuticle (outer skin) on its head forms three long points that look like a rhinoceros's horns. With all that armor, it is fairly safe for this beetle to move about!

On the Move

Beetles and bugs are expert movers. They can fly, run, leap and even swim. Some species are wingless, but most of those that have wings fly well. All adult beetles and bugs have six flexible, jointed legs, divided into four main sections. Many species have claws on their feet, which help them to cling to smooth surfaces. Others have a flat pad between the claws, with hundreds of tiny hairs. The pads allow the insects to scramble up walls and even walk upside down.

Squash bug
(*Coreus marginatus*)

▲ JOINTED LEGS

Like all beetles and bugs, squash bugs have four main sections in their legs. The top part is called the coxa, next comes the femur or upper leg, then the tibia or lower leg. The fourth section, the tarsus, is the part that touches the ground. You can also see the bug's feeding tube under its head.

▲ SPEEDY RUNNER

Tiger beetles (*Cicindela*) are one of the fastest insects—they can cover up to 2 feet a second. As it runs, the front and hind legs on one side of the beetle's body touch the ground at the same time as the middle leg on the other side. This steadies the insect, like a three-legged stool.

◄ LONG LEAPER

Leafhoppers (Cicadellidae family) are long-jump champions! When preparing to leap, the bug gathers its legs beneath it like a runner on the starting block. Muscles that connect the upper and lower leg contract (shorten) to straighten the leg and fling the bug into the air.

◄ SOIL SHIFTER

The burying, or sexton, beetle uses its strong front legs for digging. These ground-dwelling insects bury small animals (such as mice) in the ground to provide food for their young. The beetle's front legs are armed with little prongs that act as shovels, pushing the soil aside as it digs into the earth.

Burying beetle
(*Nicrophorus humator*)

ROWING THROUGH WATER ►

Pan-temperate diving beetles (*Dytiscus marginalis*) are strong swimmers. Their flattened hind legs are covered with long-haired fringes, which act like broad paddles. The two back legs push together against the water, helping the insect to "row" itself forward.

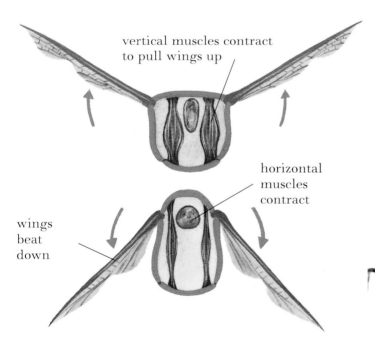

vertical muscles contract to pull wings up

horizontal muscles contract

wings beat down

◄ FLIGHT MUSCLES

Unlike flies, the beetle uses only its delicate rear wings for flying. Vertical muscles attached to the top and bottom of the thorax contract to flatten it. This makes the wings move up. Horizontal muscles along the body then contract to pull the thorax up, making the beetle's wings flip down. The action of the thorax controls the wings and propels the insect along.

Spotted longhorn
(*Strangalia maculata*)

GRACEFUL FLIER ►

A spotted longhorn beetle takes to the air. Like other insects, these beetles have two sets of flying muscles in their thorax (mid-body section). The hard front wings are held up to help steady the insect in flight. Most beetles are competent fliers, but they do not specialize in flying like some other insect species.

Beetles, bugs and other insects are the only animals without a backbone that are able to fly. They take to the air to escape from their enemies and to move from place to place in search of food. Most beetles and bugs are expert fliers.

Bugs with two pairs of wings use both sets for flying. Their front and rear wings flap up and down together. The hardened front wings of a beetle are called elytra. They are not used for powering flight but to steady the beetle as it flies. The long rear wings sweep up and down to power the beetle through the air.

1 When on the ground, the wing cases of the cockchafer beetle (*Melolontha melolontha*) meet over its body. The delicate rear wings are folded under the elytra and cannot be seen. Cockchafer beetles are also known as May bugs or June bugs, as it is in these months that they are usually seen.

2 A fire-colored beetle (*Pyrochroa serraticornis*) prepares for take-off by raising its front wings out of the way and flexing its rear flight muscles. This process checks that the wings are in good working order and warms the beetle's muscles for the flight ahead. When the warm-up is finished, the beetle is ready to go.

3 A black-tipped soldier beetle (*Rhagonycha fulva*) positions itself for take-off like a plane taxiing down a runway. It finds a breezy spot by climbing a tall plant stem. Then it balances its body on top. In this exposed place, the wind may carry it away as it raises its wings. If not, the beetle will launch itself by leaping into the air.

Beetles in Flight

4 A cockchafer maneuvers between plant stems. Its wing cases help to provide the lift it needs to remain airborne. Long rear wings provide flapping power to propel the beetle through the air. Cockchafers are clumsy fliers and sometimes stray into houses on dark evenings, drawn by the light. Indoors, the beetle may crash into objects in the unfamiliar setting, but it is so well armored that it is rarely hurt.

5 A freeze-frame photograph shows the flapping wing movements of a *Pectocera fortunei* beetle in mid-flight. These small, light beetles find it fairly easy to stay airborne. However, their small size is a disadvantage in windy conditions, when they are sometimes blown off course.

6 A cockchafer prepares to land on an oak leaf. The beetle's rear wings are angled downwards to help it lose height. As it comes in to land, the legs will move forward to take the beetle's weight on the leaf. The veins that strengthen the delicate rear wings can be clearly seen in this picture.

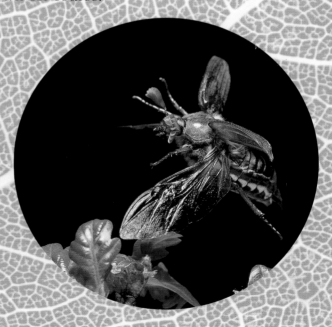

Senses

◄ SPINY SENSORS
Root-borer beetles (*Prionus coriarius*) have long, curving antennae. The antennae are covered with patterns of tiny hairs. Each hair is attached to a nerve that sends signals to the insect's brain when the hair is moved.

Beetles and bugs have keen senses, but they do not sense the world in the same way that humans do. Most beetles and bugs have good eyesight and a keen sense of smell, but no sense of hearing. The main sense organs are on the head.

Most beetles and bugs have two large eyes, called compound eyes because they are made up of many tiny lenses. These are particularly good at sensing movement. Some beetles and bugs also have simple, beadlike eyes on top of their heads, which are sensitive to light and dark.

The antennae are the main sense tools for most beetles and bugs. They are used for smelling and feeling, and in some species for hearing and tasting, too. Antennae come in various shapes—some beetles and bugs have special feelers called palps on their mouthparts.

Sensitive hairs all over the insects' bodies pick up tiny currents in the air, which may alert them to enemies nearby.

▲ BRANCHING ANTENNAE
This unusual beetle from Central America has branched antennae that look like the antlers of a stag. The branches are usually held closed, but the insect can also fan them out to pick up distant smells on the wind, such as the scent of a faraway mate. Smells such as these would be far too faint for humans to detect.

SMELL AND TOUCH ►
Longhorn beetles (Cerambycidae) are named after their long antennae. An insect's antennae are sometimes called its "feelers." The term is rather misleading—the antennae *are* used for feeling, but their main function is to pick up scents. Long antennae like the longhorn beetle's are especially sensitive to smell and touch.

◀ ELBOW-SHAPED

The weevil's antennae are found on its long nose. Many weevils have jointed antennae, which bend in the middle like a human arm at the elbow. Some have special organs at the base of their antennae, which vibrate to sound and act as ears. This brush-snouted weevil (*Rhina tarbirostris*) has a bushy "beard" of long, sensitive hairs on its snout.

COMPOUND EYES ▶

The huge eyes of the harlequin beetle (*Acrocinus longimanus*) cover its head. Only the area from which its antennae sprout remains uncovered. Each compound eye is made up of hundreds of tiny lenses. Scientists believe that the signals from each lens build up to create one large picture. Even so, scientists are not sure what beetles and bugs see.

◀ TINY LENSES

A close-up of a beetle's compound eye shows that it is made up of many tiny facets, each of which points in a slightly different direction. Each is made up of a lens at the surface and a second lens inside. The lenses focus light down a central structure inside the eye, called the rhabdome, on to a bundle of nerve fibers, which are behind the eye. The nerve fibers then send messages to the brain. The hundreds of tiny lenses probably do not create the detailed, focused image produced by the human eye. However, they can pick up colors and shapes and are very good at detecting tiny movements.

Plant Eaters and Pests

Beetles and bugs do not always eat the same food throughout their lives. Larvae often eat very different foods from their parents. Some adult beetles and bugs do not feed at all, and instead put all their energy into finding a mate and reproducing very quickly.

Most bugs and some beetles are herbivores. Different species feed on the leaves, buds, seeds and roots of plants, on tree wood or on fungi. Many plant eaters become pests when they feed on cultivated plants or crops. Other beetles and bugs are carnivores, or recycle waste by consuming dead plants or animals. Others nibble things that humans would not consider edible, such as clothes, woolen carpets, wooden furniture and even animal dung.

▲ **TUNNEL-EATERS**
This tree has been eaten by bark beetles (Scolytidae). Females lay their eggs under tree bark. When the young hatch, each eats its way through the wood to create a long, narrow tunnel just wide enough to squeeze through.

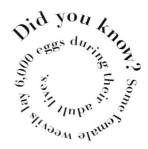

Did you know? Some female weevils lay 9,000 eggs during their adult lives.

Squash bug
(*Coreus marginatus*)

◄ **SQUASH-LOVERS**
Squash bugs are named after their favorite food. The squash family includes zucchini and pumpkins. This bug is about to nibble a zucchini flower bud. Most squash bugs are green or brown in color. They feed on the green parts of squash plants, and also on the seeds. This harms future crops. The insects are a pest in the United States.

▲ A PLAGUE OF APHIDS

Aphids are small, soft-bodied bugs. They use their sharp, beak-like mouths to pierce the stems of plants and suck out the sap inside. Aphids feed on the sap of plants, which is found in the stems and veins of leaves. These insects breed very quickly in warm weather.

▲ BEETLE ATTACK

Colorado potato beetles (*Leptinotarsa decemlineata*) are high on the list of dangerous insects in many countries. The beetles originally came from the western United States, where they ate the leaves of local plants. When European settlers came and cultivated potatoes, the beetles ate the crop and did great damage. Colorado potato beetles later spread to become a major pest in Europe, but are now controlled by pesticides.

▲ SCALY FEEDERS

Most female scale insects (Coccoidae family) have neither legs nor wings, but they can be identified as bugs from the way their mouth is formed. Scale insects are usually well camouflaged, but the species shown here can be seen clearly. They are feeding on a juicy melon by piercing the skin and sucking up the sap.

▲ THE EVIL WEEVIL

These grains of wheat have been infested by grain weevils (*Sitophilus zeamais*). The adult weevils bore through the grain's hard case with their long snouts to reach the soft kernel inside. Females lay their eggs inside the kernels. Then, when the young hatch, they can feed in safety.

Scavengers and Hunters

Ground beetle
(*Lorica pilicornis*)

▲ **SPEEDY HUNTER**
A ground beetle feeds on a juicy worm it has caught. Ground beetles are a large family of beetles, with over 20,000 species. Many species cannot fly, hence their name. However, most ground beetles are fast runners. The beetle uses its speed to overtake its fleeing victim. Once trapped, the victim is firmly grabbed in the beetle's powerful jaws.

Many beetles and some bugs are carnivores (meat eaters). Some hunt and kill live prey, others prefer their meat dead. Called scavengers, they feed on the remains of animals. Some other beetles and bugs are parasites that live on larger animals and eat their flesh, or drink their blood, without killing them.

Most predator beetles and bugs hunt fellow insects or other small creatures such as millipedes. Some tackle larger game, such as fish, tadpoles, frogs, snails and worms. Beetles and bugs use a variety of different tricks and techniques to catch and overpower their prey. Most beetles seize their victims in their jaws, and crush or crunch them up to kill them. Bugs suck their victims' juices from their bodies while they are still alive.

◄ **GONE FISHING**
Pan-temperate diving beetles (*Dytiscus marginalis*) are fierce aquatic hunters. They hunt down fish, tadpoles, newts and other creatures that live in ponds and streams. This beetle has caught a stickleback. It grabs the fish in its jaws, then injects it with digestive juices that dissolve the fish's flesh. When the victim finally stops struggling and dies, the beetle begins to feed.

▲ **VAMPIRE BEETLE**

Most assassin bugs (Reduviidae) are killers. Many species hunt small creatures and suck their juices dry. Some are parasites. The species above feeds on humans by injecting their skin with a painkiller so it can feast unnoticed.

EATEN ALIVE ▶

This shield bug (*Palomena prasina*) has caught a caterpillar. With a victim in its clutches, it uses its curving mouthparts to suck its prey dry. Most types of shield bugs are plant eaters, but some hunt living creatures. The bugs use their front legs to hold their victims steady while they feast on them.

Did you know? Great diving beetles store air under their wings when they dive.

◀ **NO ESCAPE**

A snail-hunter beetle (*Calosoma*) tackles a small snail. To protect itself, the snail retreats into its shell and seals the opening with slime. In response, the beetle squirts a liquid into the shell to dissolve the slime and kill the snail.

Escaping Danger

The naturalist Charles Darwin's theory of evolution explains how only the fittest animals survive to breed and pass on their characteristics to the next generation. The key to survival is escaping danger. Beetles and bugs have many enemies in the natural world. They also have many ways of avoiding attack. Many species run, fly, hop or swim away, but some species are also armed with weapons. Some bugs and beetles can bite or use sharp spines for protection. Others are armed with poisonous fluids or taste bad. These insects are often brightly colored, which tells predators such as birds to stay away.

▲ **PROTECTIVE SPINES**
A weevil (*Lixus barbiger*) from the island of Madagascar has an impressive array of sharp spines on its back. Few predators will try such a prickly morsel—if they do, the pain may make them drop their meal!

▲ **READY TO SHOOT**
Desert skunk beetles (*Eleodes armata*) defend themselves by shooting a foul-smelling spray from their abdomens. This beetle has taken up a defensive posture by balancing on its head with its abdomen raised in the air. It is ready to fire its spray if an intruder comes close. Most predators will back away.

▼ **WHAT A STINK**
Squash bugs (*Coreus marginatus*) are also known as stink bugs because of the smelly spray they produce to ward off enemies. Like other insects, squash bugs do not actively *decide* to defend themselves. They instinctively react when their sense organs tell them that danger is near.

Blistering Attack

The blister beetle (Meloidae) *gives off a chemical that causes human and animal skin to blister. Centuries ago, the chemical was thought to cure warts. Doctors applied blister beetles to the skin of patients suffering from the infection. The "cure" was probably painful and did not work.*

▼ TRICKY BEETLE

The devil's coach-horse beetle has several ways of defending itself from attack. First, it raises its tail in a pose that mimics a stinging scorpion (below). This defence is a trick, for the beetle cannot sting. If the trick does not work, the beetle gives off an unpleasant smell to send its enemies reeling. If all else fails, it delivers a painful bite with its large jaws.

Devil's coach-horse beetle
(Staphylinus olens)

◀ PLAYING DEAD

This weevil from East Africa is trying to fool an enemy by playing dead. It drops to the ground and lies on its back with its legs curled in a lifeless position. This defence works well on enemies that eat only live prey. However, it does not work on the many predators that are not fussy whether their victims are alive or dead.

WARNING COLORS ▶

The fire-colored beetle's body contains chemicals that have a terrible taste to predators. The beetle's blood red color helps to warn its enemies away. The color coding will only work if the predator has tried to eat another beetle of the same species. If so, it will recognize the species by its color and leave it alone.

Fire-colored beetle
(Pyrochroa coccinea)

27

FOCUS on

Ladybugs are the only insects that many people will touch because they are known to be harmless. There are more than 4,000 different types of ladybugs in temperate and tropical countries all over the world. The insects are easy to recognize because of their rounded body shape. Most ladybugs are brightly colored (red, yellow or orange) with black spots. These colors warn predators that ladybugs taste horrible.

Farmers and gardeners appreciate ladybugs because they are carnivores and feed on aphids and other insects that cause damage to crops. One ladybug can eat up to 50 aphids a day. During the late 1800s, ladybugs were used to control the cottony cushion scale (*Icerya purchasi*)—a bug that threatened to destroy all the lemon trees in California.

FLYING COLORS
The eyed ladybug (*Anatis ocellata*) is a large European species. Most ladybugs are red with black spots. Some have yellow or white spots, or multicolored markings, like this species (above). Some ladybugs have stripes instead of spots, and others are black with no markings at all.

HEADS OR TAILS?
A seven-spot ladybug (*Coccinella septempunctata*) scurries across a leaf. Like all ladybugs, its bright colors are found on the elytra (wing cases), which fold over the insect's back. The head and thorax are black. The pale markings that look like eyes are actually on the thorax.

Ladybugs

FLY AWAY HOME

A ladybug in flight shows that, like other beetles, the insect holds its wing cases out of the way when flying. In spring, ladybugs lay their eggs on plants infested with aphids. When the hungry young ladybug grubs hatch, they devour large quantities of the plant-eating pests.

HEAVEN-SENT HELPERS

A ladybug munches an aphid. Ladybugs are popular with market gardeners because they eat aphids and other insects that attack trees and crops. In medieval times, Europeans believed that ladybugs were sent by the Virgin Mary to help farmers—hence the name ladybug.

WINTER SLEEP

Ladybugs cluster on a twig in winter. They survive the cold by entering a deep sleep called hibernation. They hibernate together in large numbers, in sheds, cellars or under tree bark. Collectors use this period to harvest large quantities of the beetles to sell to suppliers and garden shops for pest control.

Natural Disguises

Many beetles and bugs have colors and patterns on their bodies that disguise them in the natural world. Such disguises are called camouflage and hide the insects from their predators. Various species imitate natural objects, including sticks, grass, seeds, bark and thorns. Others are disguised as unpleasant objects, such as animal droppings, which predators avoid when looking for food.

Some beetles and bugs have another clever way of surviving—they mimic the color or shape of insects such as wasps and ants that are poisonous or can sting. Predators recognize and avoid the warning signs of the harmless imitators, mistaking them for the dangerous insects.

▲ BLADERUNNER
The top of this grass stem is actually a damsel bug (*Stenodema laengatum*) posing as a blade of grass. This bug's camouflage helps it to hide from its enemies — *and* sneak up on its prey, for the damsel bug is also a fierce predator.

Wasp beetle
(*Clytus arietis*)

▲ STRIPY WARNING
This beetle's bold black-and-yellow stripes suggest it is a wasp, armed with a painful sting. Although the insect is harmless, the warning colors are enough to put most predators off.

UNDER COVER ▶
A group of female scale insects (Coccoidae family) feed on a bay tree, disguised by their camouflage. The bugs also produce a bad-tasting waxy white substance around their bodies. In this way, they can feed without being attacked by their enemies.

THORNY PROBLEM ▶

The sharp thorns on this twig look like part of the plant. They are, in fact, thorn bugs (*Umbonia crassicornus*). Each bug perfects its disguise by pointing in the same direction as the others on the twig. If they pointed in different directions, the bugs would look less like part of the plant. Even if a predator does spot the bugs, their prickly spines deter any passing enemy.

◀ **ANT COSTUME**

This treehopper (*Cyphonia clavata*) from the West Indies is a master of disguise. Its green body and transparent wings make it almost invisible when feeding on leaves. In addition, it has an amazing black ant disguise on its back, which can be seen clearly by predators. True ants are armed with biting jaws and can also squirt stinging acid at their enemies. Predators will avoid them at all costs, and so the insect's clever disguise allows it to feed without being disturbed.

EYE SPY ▶

Click beetles have mottled colors that help them to blend in with grass or tree bark. The big-eyed click beetle (*Alaus oculatus*, right) has two large eyespots on its thorax. These resemble the eyes of a large predator, such as an owl. These frightening markings will be enough to stop any predatory bird from attacking the beetle.

Focus on

FIREFLY ANATOMY
Fireflies are flat and slender.
Most are dark brown or
black, with orange or yellow
markings. The light organs
are found in their abdomens.
Most species have two sets of
wings, but in some, the
females have no wings at all.

At nightfall in warm countries, the darkness
may be lit up by hundreds of tiny green-yellow
lights. The lights are produced by insects called
fireflies, also known as glow worms. There are
over 1,000 different types of fireflies, but not all
species glow in the dark. The light is produced
by special organs in the insects' abdomens.
Fireflies are nocturnal (night-active) beetles.
Some species produce a continuous greenish
glow, others flash their lights on and off. These
signals are all designed for one purpose—to
attract a mate.

PRODUCING LIGHT
A male firefly flashes his light to females nearby.
He produces light when chemicals mix in his abdomen,
causing a reaction that releases energy in the form
of light. In deep oceans, many sea creatures produce
light in a similar way, including fish and squid.

CODED SIGNALS
A female firefly climbs onto a grass stem to
signal with her glowing tail. Each species of
firefly has its own sequence of flashes, which
serves as a private mating code. On warm
summer evenings, the wingless females send
this code to the flashing males that fly above.

Fireflies

FALSE CODE

Most adult fireflies feed on flower nectar or do not eat at all. However, the female of this North American species is a meat eater—and her prey is other fireflies. When the flightless female sees a male firefly of a different species circling overhead, she flashes his response code to attract him to the ground. When he lands nearby, she pounces and eats him. She also flashes to males of her own species to attract them to her for mating.

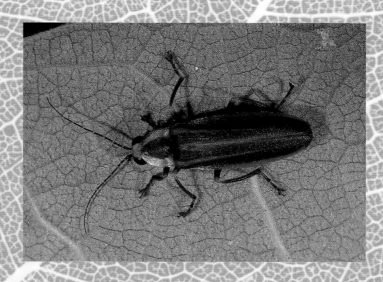

PULSE OF LIGHT

A group of fireflies light up a tree by a bridge as they signal to one another. In parts of Asia, some species of fireflies gather in large groups on trees. When one insect, called a pacemaker, flashes its light, all the other fireflies on the tree begin to flash their lights at the same time and to the same pattern. When this happens, the whole tree can be seen to glow and pulse with brilliant flashes of light.

YOUNG FIREFLIES

Like the adults, firefly larvae also make light. It is only the young, wingless insects and the flightless females that are called glow worms. Young fireflies hatch from eggs laid in moist places by the females. Unlike most of their parents, all firefly larvae are meat eaters. They kill slugs and snails by injecting them with poison. The young insects use their sharp jaws to hook the snails out of their shells and then gobble them up.

Attracting a Mate

One of the most important tasks for any animal is to continue its species by breeding. Beetles and bugs are no exception, and most must mate before they produce young.

Many beetles and bugs use scent to attract the opposite sex. They give off special smells that can travel a long distance through the air. The opposite sex then follow the trail of scent to find a partner to mate with. Some species use sound to attract a mate that is far away.

At close quarters, beetles and bugs may partly identify one another by sight. If two or more males are attracted to one female, the rivals may fight for the chance to mate. In some species, males and females spend several hours courting—checking that they have found a suitable mate. In other species, mating takes only a few minutes, after which the two insects go their separate ways.

▲ **IRRESISTIBLE SMELL**
Bark beetles (Scolytidae) live in tree trunks. Females of some species produce a scent, which male beetles pick up using their antennae. Sometimes, many males are drawn to just one female.

Did you know? Most beetles mate for only a few seconds but some mate for hours.

Rhododendron leafhopper
(Graphocephala fennahi)

◄ **SOUND SIGNALS**
Male leafhopper bugs "sing" to attract their partners. They produce little squeaks and rasping sounds by rubbing their wings against their abdomen. The female insects have special hearing organs that can detect the high-pitched calls made by their mates. The sounds are far too quiet for humans to hear.

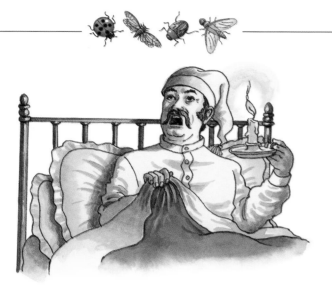

Ominous Sound

Deathwatch beetles (Xestobium rufovillosum) live in rotting logs and also in wooden buildings. During the breeding season, they tap on the wood at night to attract a mate. These sounds, sometimes heard by sick people awake at night, were once thought to be very unlucky. The tapping was believed to be an omen of death—hence the beetle's name.

▲ SPOTTING A MATE

Seven-spot ladybugs (*Coccinella septempunctata*) mate on a leaf. The male mounts the female to release sperm to fertilize her eggs. Ladybugs use sight to identify one another. They are guided to their own species by the different numbers of spots on their elytra (wing cases). Once they have found one of their own kind, they can mate successfully to produce young.

◀ FROG LEGS

This athletic-looking insect is a Malayan frog beetle. The species owes its name to the male beetle's powerful, froglike hind legs. The insect uses his legs for leaping, but also for breeding. He clings onto the female beetle during mating, which helps to make sure that the union is fertile.

Malayan frog beetle
(*Sagra buqueti*)

▲ MALE AND FEMALE

A male aphid mates with a female. Many male and female beetles and bugs look similar to one another, but some aphids are different. The females have plump, green bodies. The males are thinner, with dark bodies and large wings. There are more female aphids than males. Males appear only in autumn, to mate with the females. The females lay fertilized eggs, which survive the winter and hatch in spring.

Focus on Stag

Courtship is a risky business for some types of beetles. Males will fight to mate with a female—sometimes to the death. Stag beetles (*Lucanus cervus*) are fighting beetles. They owe their name to the huge jaws of the male, which resemble a stag's antlers. The female stag beetle releases a scent which attracts males to her. Males can sense this scent from up to half a mile away. If two rival males appear, they may fight. Each beetle tries to hoist his rival in the air and smash him to the ground.

1 A male stag beetle displays his fearsome horns, which can be as long as his body. The beetle uses its jaws not for feeding, but to frighten away rival males and predators.

2 Like the male stag beetle, the body of the female is well armored. Her jaws are much smaller than the male's, however, and are not designed for fighting. The female's main purpose is to survive long enough to breed.

3 Two male beetles size each other up on the prime breeding ground of an old tree stump. Each male tries to frighten the other with his giant horns. If neither beetle backs down and scuttles away, the fight will start.

Beetle Contests

4 The rival males begin to wrestle. As they lock horns, each tries to gain the upper hand by gripping his enemy. The fierce-looking jaws rarely do serious damage, but the fight tests the strength and endurance of both insects.

5 The strongest beetle grips his enemy in his jaws and lifts him high. The other beetle is helpless in this position, but the victor struggles to keep his balance. One slip and the other beetle could take control.

6 The victorious beetle ends the contest by dashing his rival to the ground, or by throwing him off the log. If the loser lands on his back, he may be unable to get up—particularly if he is wounded. The defeated beetle may well be eaten alive by predatory insects, such as ants. The strongest male wins his right to mate with the female, and so pass on his characteristics to the next generation. This process ensures that only the strongest genes are passed on, guaranteeing the survival of the fittest.

The Life Cycle of Beetles

▲ **LAYING EGGS**

A female fire-colored beetle (*Pyrochroa coccinea*) lays its eggs in dead wood. The hard tip of the beetle's abdomen pierces the wood to lay the eggs inside. When the eggs hatch, the log provides the larvae with a hiding place from predators. They feast on the timber until they are fully grown.

Beetles and bugs have different life cycles. During their lives, beetles pass through four stages. From eggs, they hatch into larvae (young) called grubs. The grubs do not look like their parents. Some have legs, but many look like long, pale worms. They all live in different places from the adults and eat different food.

Beetle larvae are hungry feeders. They feed, grow and moult their skins several times, but do not change form or grow wings. When the larva is fully grown, it develops a hard case and enters a resting stage, called a pupa. Inside the case, the grub's body is totally dissolved and then rebuilt. It emerges from its pupa as a winged adult. This amazing process is called complete metamorphosis. The word "metamorphosis" means transformation.

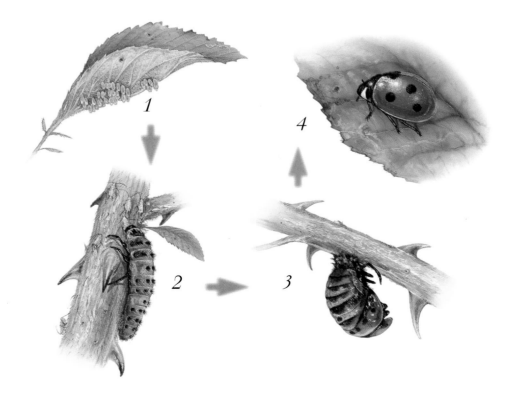

◄ **THE FOUR STAGES**

There are four stages in a beetle's life cycle. It begins life as an egg (1), then becomes a larva or grub (2). The full-grown larva then becomes a pupa (3) before it reaches adulthood (4). At each stage, the beetle's appearance is almost totally different from the last stage. In a way, a developing beetle is several animals in one. When the beetle finally emerges from its pupa as an adult, it is ready to breed, and so the life cycle can begin again.

◄ BEETLE EGGS

The female ladybug glues her eggs onto leaves so that they stand on end. Beetle eggs are generally rounded or oval. They are usually yellow, green or black for camouflage. Most eggs are laid in spring or summer, and most hatch between one week and one month later. Some eggs are laid in autumn and hatch the following spring. They take longer to hatch because of the cooler conditions.

LARVA ►

This cockchafer larva (*Melolontha melolontha*) looks nothing like the adult. Its long, fat body is very different from the adult's rounded shape. However, unlike many beetle grubs, it does have legs. The larva has no compound eyes or long antennae. Nor does it have wings, but moves about by wriggling its way through the soil.

◄ PUPA

When a beetle grub is fully grown, it attaches itself to a plant stem or hides underground. Then it develops a hard outer case to become a pupa. Unlike the grub, the pupa doesn't feed or move much. It looks dead, but inside its hard case, an amazing change is taking place. The insect's body breaks down into a kind of soup, and is reshaped into an adult beetle.

ADULT FORM ►

An adult seven-spotted ladybug (*Coccinella septempunctata*) struggles out of its pupa case. It emerges complete with long, jointed legs, wings and antennae. Its yellow wing cases will develop spots after just a few hours. Some beetles spend only a week as pupae before emerging as fully grown adults. Others pass the whole winter in the resting stage, waiting to emerge until the following spring.

The Life Cycle of Bugs

Bugs develop in a different way from beetles. Most bugs hatch from eggs laid by females after mating. Newly hatched bugs are called nymphs and look like tiny adults, but they are wingless. Nymphs often eat the same food and live in the same places as their parents.

Unlike human skin, an insect's exoskeleton is not stretchy. Nymphs are hungry eaters, and as they feed and grow, their hard skins become too tight and must be shed several times. This process is called molting. The nymphs then develop new skins, inside which there is space to grow. As they grow, they gradually sprout wings. After a final molt, the bugs emerge as winged adults. This process is called incomplete metamorphosis because, unlike beetles, bugs do not go through the pupa stage and totally rebuild their bodies.

▲ **BUG EGGS**
Like other young insects, most bugs start out as eggs. These little yellow balls are shield bug eggs (*Eysarcoris fabricii*). They are all at various stages of development. The yellow eggs on the left are more developed than the paler eggs on the right, and will soon hatch into young.

Did you know? In summer, female aphids give birth to up to 50 young in a week.

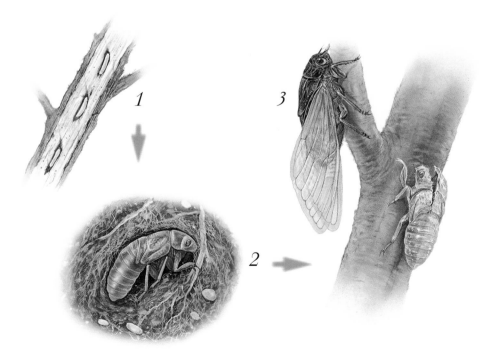

1

3

2

◄ **THE THREE STAGES**
There are three different stages in a bug's life. The first stage is the egg (1), from which the bug hatches as a nymph (2). The nymph gradually grows and molts a number of times. At each molt it becomes more like an adult. The wing buds appear after several molts, and gradually lengthen as the nymph reaches adulthood (3).

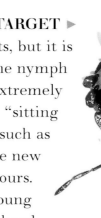

EASY TARGET ▶

This young shield bug looks like its parents, but it is wingless and cannot fly. After molting, the nymph has no hard skin to protect it and is extremely vulnerable. At this stage, young bugs are "sitting ducks," and many fall victim to predators such as lizards and birds. After molting, the new exoskeleton hardens within just a few hours. With luck, this new layer will protect the young bug for long enough to reach adulthood.

◀ FOAMY HIDEOUT

Some nymphs have special ways of avoiding predators. This froghopper nymph (*Philaemus spumarius*) hides inside the unpleasant-looking foam behind it, known as "spittle." The bug produces the froth itself by giving off a sticky liquid, which it blows into a foam. The spittle makes a good hiding place from predators, and also screens the bug from the sun.

YOUNG HUNTER ▶

Just a few hours after hatching, a young water strider (*Gerris najas*, right) begins to live and feed on the water's surface, just like its parents. A water strider's feet are covered in dense water-repellent hair, which allows it to walk on the surface of the water. Water striders are expert predators, catching other water creatures and then feeding by sucking out the victims' juices with their long feeding tubes.

◀ BREEDING WITHOUT MALES

In autumn, male and female aphids breed and lay eggs in the normal way. In summer, however, female aphids can reproduce without males, and give birth to live offspring without mating or even laying eggs. This aphid (left) is giving birth to a fully formed young. This amazing process is called parthenogenesis (meaning virgin birth.) The babies grow up quickly, and can themselves breed after just one week.

41

▲ SOIL DWELLERS

Click beetle larvae (Elateridae family) are called wireworms. They have wormlike bodies and tiny legs. Most are bright yellow or orange. Wireworms live in soil and feed on the roots of grasses. They can cause damage to crops by eating their roots.

▲ LIVELY LARVA

A ladybug larva (*Coccinella septempunctata*) munches aphids. Many grubs are legless or not quick on their feet, but young ladybugs are nimble and lively, like tiny lizards.

UNDER DUNG ▶

Beetles that live above ground need to find some way to protect themselves from enemies. This green tortoise beetle larva (*Cassida viridis*) is hiding from predators by carrying a lump of dung on its tail.

Young Beetles

The main purpose of an adult beetle is to reproduce. The goal for a larva is to reach adulthood, which they do by feeding, growing, and avoiding predators. Most beetles lay their eggs on or near a suitable food source for their young, such as dead wood, plants or even in a living animal.

Various species of beetles spend different amounts of time as eggs, larvae, pupae and adults. Ladybugs spend just one week as an egg, three to six weeks as larvae and then another week as pupae. Stag beetles take longer to grow. They hatch after two weeks as an egg, but then spend up to five years as grubs living in dead wood and another eight months as pupae. Adult stag beetles live only a few months before they die.

▲ WOODBORERS

Metallic woodboring beetles (Buprestidae) live in tunnels in dead wood. The larvae feed on the timber, but it is not very nourishing. So the young grubs must spend many years feeding before they are ready to pupate and become adults. One type of metallic woodboring beetle spends 40 years in the timber before it is fully grown.

Deadly Beetle

The pupae of a particular kind of South African leaf beetle produce a deadly poison. Just the smallest trace of the poison can kill a large animal, such as a gazelle. Kalahari bushmen tip the points of their arrows with the beetle's poison before going on hunting trips. Preparing their weapons is very dangerous. The hunters take great care to make sure that the poison does not get into cuts or grazes on their own skin. If it does, they could die.

▲ HIDDEN TRAP

The tiger beetle larva (*Cicindela*) is a stealthy predator. It makes a burrow in the soil and fills the entrance with its huge jaws. It then waits until a passing insect comes close enough to grab. The beetle's jaws snap shut and it drags its prey into its burrow to finish it off.

FREE AT LAST ▶

A nut weevil larva (*Curculio nucum*) pokes its head out of a hazel nut. Its mother drilled into the nut to lay her egg inside. The grub hatched and fed inside the nut, then gnawed its way to freedom. It will not spend long in the open air. Instead, it will quickly burrow into the soil, where it will pupate.

Caring for the Young

Oak roller weevil
(*Attelebus nitens*)

Most beetles and bugs do not actively care for their offspring. They simply lay their eggs on a suitable food source, and then leave the young to fend for themselves. A few species, though, are caring parents. Some beetles, such as oak roller weevils, take great effort to protect their eggs. Other species, such as burying beetles, feed their larvae themselves.

Cross-winged bugs, such as shield bugs, guard and watch over their nymphs until the babies become big enough to look after themselves. Passalid beetles take even greater care of their young. Like ants, termites, and some bees and wasps, they are social insects. Social insects live and work together in a group. These beetle parents, and even their older offspring, take great pains to rear their young.

▲ SAFE HOME

Oak roller weevils lay their eggs high up in oak trees. The females use their jaws to snip the oak leaves into sections. They then curl the leaves into tight rolls, in which they lay their eggs. Inside the rolls, the eggs are safe from predators that might eat the eggs or feed them to their own young.

CARING MOM ▶

A female shield bug, known as the parent bug (*Elasmucha grisea*), protects her young from a predatory spider. Her large brood of nymphs cluster behind her for safety. A distant relative, the male giant water bug, protects his eggs by carrying them on his body until they hatch.

Did you know? Some water beetles weave a web around the eggs to keep them dry.

Sacred Scarabs

Scarab beetles were sacred to the ancient Egyptians. They symbolized the sun god, Ra. Each day, Ra rolled the fiery ball of the sun across the sky, just as the scarab beetle rolls a ball of dung to a suitable place to lay its eggs. The scarab beetle was a symbol of rebirth, and it was used to decorate tombs and many sacred objects.

◄ DUNG-ROLLERS

Dung beetles are part of the scarab beetle family (Scarabaeidae). These beetles and their young feed on the droppings of mammals such as buffalo. To provide for the young, the male and female beetles shape the dung into a ball. They then roll it to a safe place, where they bury it. The female beetle lays her eggs in the dung ball. When the young hatch, they will have a ready food supply in a safe hiding hole. The buried dung also helps to fertilize the soil.

▲ FAMILY GROUPS

Bessbugs live in families. They inhabit rotting tree trunks, in a maze of tunnels. These parent beetles are tending pupae in their white cocoons. When the pupae emerge as adults, they stay in the nest to help rear the next generation of young.

▲ PERSONAL CARE

A burying beetle (*Nicrophorus humator*) crawls over a dead shrew. The parent beetles tunnel under the dead body to bury it. The female then lays her eggs on the animal. Some beetles wait for the young to hatch, then feed them the meat of the dead mammal themselves.

45

Homes and Habitats

Around the world, beetles and bugs are found in all sorts of different habitats. Most live in hot, tropical regions or in mild, temperate areas. Many beetles and bugs are found in places that have moderate or heavy rainfall, but some tough species manage to live in deserts. Others can survive on snow-capped mountains or frozen icefields, in caves, sewers and even hot springs.

Beetles and bugs that live in very cold or very hot places must be able to cope with extreme temperatures. Many survive the harsh weather as pupae, or as eggs in the soil. In deserts, most species are active at night, when the air is cooler. The toughest species can go for long periods without food or even water. These insects are small enough to shelter from storms or predators in tiny nooks and crannies.

▲ **PARASITES**
Bedbugs (*Cimex lectularius*) are parasites that live and feed on warm-blooded animals. Some species suck human blood. Bedbugs that infest birds and furry mammals live in their nests, or among their feathers or hair. Kept warm by their host animal, some bedbugs can even survive in cold places such as the Arctic.

Did you know? Water boatmen can fly many kilometres to find a new home.

◀ **UPSIDE-DOWN WORLD**
Back swimmers (*Notonecta maculata*) live upside-down in water. The bug hangs just below the water surface, and uses its oarlike legs to move about, rather like rowing. Like many bugs that live in water, the boatman is a hunter. It grabs small creatures that have fallen into the water, and sucks their juices dry.

LONG LIMBS ▶

This stilt-legged bug (Berytidae) lives in caves in the Caribbean. Its long, thin legs and antennae help it to feel its way in the dark. The legs and antennae are also covered with hairs that can detect the slightest air currents, alerting the bug to the presence of other animals.

◀ **DESERT SURVIVOR**

The fog-basking beetle (*Onymachris unguicularis*) lives in the Namib Desert, in southern Africa. This beetle has an ingenious way of drinking. When fog and mist swirl over the dunes, it does a handstand and points its abdomen in the air. Moisture gathers on its body, then trickles down special grooves on its back into its waiting mouth.

SURVIVING IN CAVES ▶

This beetle (*Aphaenops*) lives in caves high in the Pyrenees Mountains, between France and Spain. Its body is not well camouflaged, but in the darkness of the caves, disguise is not important. Scientists believe some cave-dwelling species developed from beetles that first lived in the caves during the last Ice Age, about a million years ago.

◀ **DUNE DWELLER**

The dune beetle (*Onymacris bocolor*) lives in the deserts of southern Africa. It is one of the few white beetles. White reflects the rays of the sun and helps to keep the insect cool. The pale color also blends in well with the sand where it lives, which helps it to hide from predators. The beetle's elytra (wing cases) are hard and close-fitting, and so help to conserve (keep) precious body moisture in this dry region. Long legs raise the beetle's body above the burning desert sand.

Tropical Beetles and Bugs

An amazing range of beetles and bugs live in tropical countries, where the weather is always hot. In this climate, these cold-blooded insects can stay active all year round. Parts of the tropics have dense rainforests and this wealth of plant food means that rainforests contain more types of beetles and bugs than any other habitat on Earth. A single rainforest tree may hold several thousand different kinds of insects. Some beetles and bugs live high in the treetops. Others live among the tangled vegetation halfway up tall trees, or among the decaying plants and fungi of the forest floor.

The tropical regions are home to many brightly colored beetles and bugs. Other species wear subtle colors that blend in with their home.

▲ BRIGHT BUG

Tropical shield bugs (Heteroptera order) come in many bright colors. Some are warning colors, which tell predators that these insects can defend themselves. This shield bug nymph from Indonesian can also produce a foul smell if attacked.

Did you know? Cicadas that live in moist places coat their bodies with a waterproof wax.

◄ UNDER COVER

Most metallic woodboring beetles (Buprestidae family) are known for their bright, rainbow colors, but this species from southern Africa is more subtly colored. The hairs on the beetle's thorax add to its disguise, and may help repel attackers. Its bright, shiny relatives are often prized by collectors. Sometimes these unfortunate insects are actually made into jewelery.

◀ BEAUTIFUL BEETLE

Tropical rainforests are home to some of the world's most spectacular beetles. Few are more splendid than this golden beetle from Central America. Surprisingly, the beetle's shiny colors work as camouflage. The insect looks like a raindrop glinting in the sun, so its enemies don't notice it. The colors are created when sunlight bounces off the insect's skin.

LURKING HUNTER ▶

This colorful assassin bug (Reduviidae) is from Africa. Like most of its family, it lies in wait for small creatures, then sucks its victims dry. The bug can be seen clearly on a dark leaf, but it is well camouflaged in the tropical flowers and stems among which it hides. The eyespots on its back scare away enemies.

◀ CLOWN BUG

A harlequin bug from southern Africa rests on a tree seed. These bugs are named after clowns called harlequins, who wear costumes with bright patterns. In Australia, male, female and young harlequins are all different brilliant colors—red, yellow or blue with green spots. Some harlequin species make their homes high in the treetops.

BARK MIMIC ▶

A longhorn beetle (Cerambycidae) from southwest Africa demonstrates the power of camouflage. The beetle's feelers and its square shape resemble the cracks and flaking texture of the tree bark, making it almost invisible. Its long antennae are spread wide to pick up scents in the wind.

Focus on

Cicadas are sometimes called locusts or harvest flies, but they are neither. These insects are bugs that live in the tropics and warm countries. They are well known for their noisy "songs," which the males produce to attract a mate.

Like other bugs, cicadas undergo incomplete metamorphosis to become adults. Some species live longer than most other insects—periodical cicadas can be 17 years old before they reach adulthood. The bugs survive beneath the ground by gnawing on plant roots.

BIG BUG

Most cicadas are large insects and can be more than 1½ inches long. This giant cicada from Africa is even bigger and has a wingspan of 6 inches.

RED EYE

This cicada from Australia is sucking plant sap. Its long, strawlike mouthparts pierce the plant stem. It has large red eyes—hence its name, red-eye cicada (*Psaltodea moerens*).

SINGING FOR A MATE

Male cicadas sing "courtship songs" to attract females. When the male flexes muscles in his abdomen, two thin, drum-like sheets of skin on the sides of the abdomen vibrate to make a stream of clicking sounds.

Cicadas

LAYING EGGS

After mating, the female cicada lays her eggs on a twig. She uses the sharp tip of the egg-layer on her abdomen to cut slits in the bark for hundreds of tiny eggs. The nymphs hatch about six weeks later. They drop to the ground and burrow into the soil to develop.

FINAL MOLT

When the cicada nymph is fully grown, it climbs out of the soil and clambers up a tree trunk for its final molt. This is an amazing sight. The back of the cicada's old skin bursts apart, and the young adult slowly struggles out. This bug is a dogday cicada (*Tibicen canicularis*), a species from North America. While it does not live quite as long as the periodical cicada, this nymph spends up to seven years underground before becoming an adult.

SPREAD YOUR WINGS

As the dogday cicada scrambles clear of its old skin, its wings uncurl and lengthen. The bug spreads its wings out to dry. Until it can fly, it is an easy target for birds and lizards. The young adults fly off to sing for a few weeks before they die. During their brief adult lives, they will mate and lay eggs, so that a new generation of bugs will emerge from the soil.

Temperate Beetles and Bugs

The world's temperate regions lie north and south of the tropics. Temperate lands have a mild climate, with warm summers and cold winters. When trees and plants lose their leaves in winter, food is scarce for beetles and bugs, and many adult insects die. Their eggs or pupae survive to hatch in the spring. The natural vegetation of temperate regions is grassland or woodland. These rich food sources ensure that temperate lands are home to thousands of beetle and bug species.

Green shield bug
(*Palomena prasina*)

▲ SPITTING BLOOD

Bloody-nosed beetles (*Timarcha tenebricosa*) are large, slow-moving insects. Their striking black color can attract unwelcome attention. To protect itself, this beetle has a secret weapon — it can spurt a bright red liquid from its mouth. Most predators will leave the beetle alone if faced with this frightening sight.

▲ GREEN SHIELD BUG

This shield bug lives on trees and shrubs. Towards autumn, its bright green color turns reddish brown, matching the leaves it lives on. The shield bug goes into hibernation for the winter and when it re-emerges in the spring, its bright green color will have returned. There are a number of types of shield bug. The gorse shield bug (*Piezodorus lituratus*) is red only as a young adult. After hibernation, it becomes yellow-green.

Hairy click beetle
(Athous hirtus)

◄ CLEVER CLICK

Click beetles get their name from the clicking sound they make. The beetle hooks its thorax together by locking a peg into a hole on its belly. When the peg is released with a click, it throws the beetle into the air, helping it to escape from enemies. The beetle also uses the click mechanism to right itself if it falls on its back.

WILD ROVER ►

Rove beetles (Staphylinidae family) are a large beetle family, with more than 20,000 species. They are found in tropical and temperate lands worldwide. With their long, slim bodies, some species look like earwigs. Others are very hairy. Most species lurk under stones or in the soil.

Rove beetle
(Creophilus maxillosus)

◄ INSECT PARTNERS

Aphids produce a sweet liquid called honeydew – a favorite food of many ants. These ants are collecting honeydew from aphids on a foxglove. Some types of ants keep aphids in the same way that people keep cattle. They "milk" the aphids by stroking them with their antennae. This makes the aphids release their honeydew. In return, the ants protect the aphids from ladybugs, and sting the aphids' enemies if they attack.

CARDINAL BEETLE ►

The cardinal beetle is recognizable by its distinctive, bright red elytra (wing cases). Adults are usually found on flowering shrubs or tree trunks. The females lay their eggs under the dry bark of trees. When the eggs grow into larvae, they eat other insects that live in the tree. If the larvae cannot find food, they feed upon each other.

Cardinal beetle
(Pyrochroa coccinea)

53

Focus on Living

Some beetles and bugs live in and on fresh water—not only ponds and rivers but also icy lakes, mountain streams, muddy pools and stagnant marshes. Most of the larvae live in the water, where rich stocks of food make good nurseries.

Different types of beetles and bugs live at different depths in the water. Some live on the water surface or just below it. Other species swim in the mid-depths, or lurk in the mud or sand at the bottom. Beetles and bugs that live underwater carry a supply of air down with them so that they can breathe.

SURFACE SPINNERS

Whirligig beetles (*Gyrinus natator*) are oval, flattened beetles that live on the surface of ponds and streams. Their compound eyes are divided into two halves, designed to see above and below the water. When swimming, they move in circles, like spinning toys called whirligigs.

SKATING ON WATER

Water striders (*Gerris lacustris*) live on the water's surface. They move about like ice skaters, buoyed up by their light bodies. The bugs' legs make dimples on the surface of the water, but do not break it. When these bugs sense a drowning insect nearby, they skate over in gangs to feed on it.

SPINY STRAW

Water scorpions have long spines on their abdomens like true scorpions. The spines have no sting, but are used to suck air from the surface. Sensors on the spine tell the bug when it is too deep to breathe.

in Water

THE SCORPION STRIKES

Water scorpions (*Nepa cinerea*) are fierce predators. This bug has seized a stickleback fish in its pincer-like front legs. It then uses its mouthparts to pierce the fish's skin and suck its juices dry. Compared to some aquatic insects, water scorpions are not strong swimmers. They sometimes move about underwater by walking along water plants.

AIR SUPPLY

Saucer bugs (*Ilyacoris*) are expert divers. In order to breathe, the bug takes in air through spiracles (holes) in its body. Tiny bubbles of air are also trapped between the bug's body hairs, giving it its silvery color. Saucer bugs use their front legs to grab their prey. They cannot fly, but move from pond to pond by crawling through the grass.

DIVING DOWN

You can often see water boatmen (*Corixa punctata*) just below the water surface, but they can also dive below. They use their back legs to row underwater, and breathe air trapped under their wings. The females lay their eggs on water plants or glue them to stones on the stream bed. The eggs hatch two months later.

Other Insects

Many species of insects are often thought of as beetles or bugs. They may look similar or have similar habits, but scientists believe they are different enough to put them in a different order. For example, true flies (Diptera) go through a complete metamorphis, just like beetles. However, they only have one pair of wings, instead of two.

Over the next few pages we look at some of the other orders of insects and investigate the characteristics that make them unique.

There are some features that all insects share. All insects have a head, a thorax and an abdomen, and three pairs of legs. They have antennae and compound eyes. Almost all insects hatch from eggs.

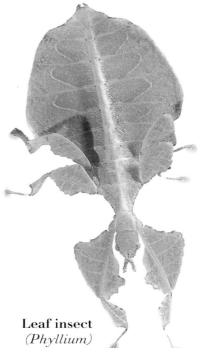

Leaf insect
(Phyllium)

▲ STICK AND LEAF INSECTS

Leaf insects resemble leaves or bark. Stick insects, which belong to the same order, look like twigs with their long, thin legs and bodies.

INSECT ORDERS ▶

This illustration shows 20 of the major insect orders, with each order represented by a particular insect. Some scientists have identified less than 25 orders, some more than 30. Some orders contain several familiar insects.

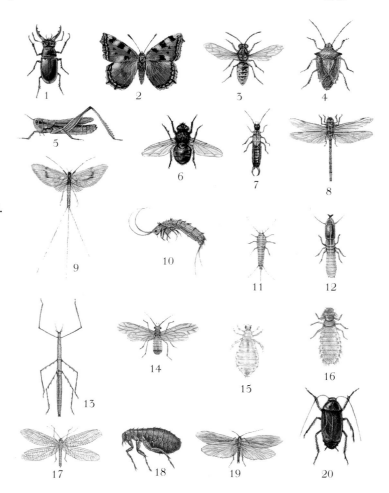

1. Coleoptera: beetle
2. Lepidoptera: butterfly
3. Hymenoptera: wasp
4. Hemiptera: shield bug
5. Orthoptera: grasshopper
6. Diptera: fly
7. Dermaptera: earwig
8. Odonata: dragonfly
9. Ephemeroptera: mayfly
10. Collembola: springtail
11. Thysanura: silverfish
12. Isoptera: termite
13. Phasmida: stick insect
14. Psocoptera: bark lice
15. Anoplura: sucking lice
16. Mallophaga: biting lice
17. Neuroptera: lacewing
18. Siphonaptera: flea
19. Trichoptera: caddisfly
20. Dictyoptera: cockroach

◄ CADDISFLIES

This strange creature is a caddisfly larva. It belongs to the Trichoptera order, which means "hair wings." The adults have two pairs of hairy, flimsy wings and look similar to moths. Their larvae grow up in ponds and streams, protected by silk cocoons and camouflaged with sticks and stones. The caddisfly larva undergoes a complete metamorphosis to become an adult.

COCKROACHES ►

Cockroaches belong to the order Dictyoptera, which means "net wings." They live in forests, caves and people's homes. Cockroaches hide by day and come out at night to feed. Once inside a house, it can be difficult to get rid of them.

Did you know? Some female earwigs lick their eggs to keep them free of infection.

Earwig
(Forficula auriculariam)

◄ EARWIGS

The Dermaptera order, which means "skin wings," includes earwigs (left). These insects' abdomens end in a pair of long, fierce pincers. Their young hatch as nymphs. Insects in the Dermaptera order have slim, brown bodies and two pairs of wings. Their long rear wings are usually folded under the short, leathery skin-like front wings, which have earned them their name.

LICE ►

Lice are parasitic insects that live on birds and mammals. They make up several orders, including biting (Mallophaga) and sucking (Anoplura) lice. All are wingless. Head lice, shown here, are sucking lice. They live and lay their eggs, called nits, in human hair.

True Flies

After beetles, flies are one of the largest insect orders. Over 90,000 different kinds of fly have been identified, including gnats, midges and mosquitoes. These hardy insects live almost everywhere on Earth, including the icy polar regions. Unlike beetles and bugs, flies have only one pair of wings. This is reflected in their order name, Diptera, which means "two wings." All that remains of the fly's hind wings are two little organs called halteres. These help the fly to balance and steer as it flies.

Ever unpopular, flies are considered dirty and carry diseases that can infect our food. Flies do have their uses, however. They fertilize flowers, and feed on dung and dead animals, reducing this waste around the world.

▲ FEEDING

This house fly is feeding on a piece of jelly. Taste sensors on its feet help it to detect its food. Like many kinds of flies, houseflies have mouths that work like sponges. They suck, or lick up, liquid foods such as sap and fruit juice. Some flies even feed on dung, rotting meat or blood.

Did you know? Over 10,000 species of crane flies are known to exist world wide.

House fly
(Musca domestica)

INSECT ACROBATS ▶

This house fly is walking upside-down across the ceiling. Many flies have hooks and sticky pads on their feet, which help them to grip smooth surfaces. Their halteres (balancing organs) make them acrobatic fliers. They can hover, fly backwards and even land upside-down. Such skills help them to dodge flyswatters.

▲ THIN AND FAT

Flies come in different shapes and sizes. Craneflies (*Tipulidae*) such as the one above, are slim and delicate. Bluebottles and house flies are stout and chunky. Some flies are ½nd-inch long—tinier than a pinhead. Others can measure a hundred times that size.

The Fly

This picture is taken from the horror film The Fly. *In the film, a scientist turns into a fly after an experiment goes wrong. Gruesome special effects make the film particularly scary. The theme proved so popular with audiences that several different versions have been made.*

▲ FOUR-STEP LIVES

Young flies are known as maggots. Like beetles, flies have four stages in their life cycle. They begin life as eggs, laid by the females in water, rotting plants or meat, or on animals. The eggs hatch into legless maggots (grubs). Later the maggots pupate to become adult flies.

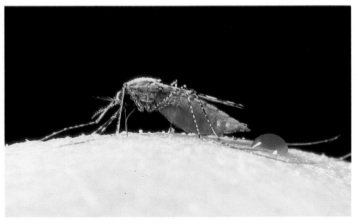

▲ CARRYING DISEASES

Mosquitoes (Culicdae) suck human and animal blood. This one is feeding from a human being. Using its needlelike mouthparts, the mosquito pierces its victim's skin to suck up blood. These insects can infect their prey with deadly diseases, including malaria and yellow fever.

Dragonflies

The order Odonata contains dragonflies and damselflies. It is a small order with just 5,000 species in total. Dragonflies and damselflies are found wetlands worldwide, both tropical and temperate. Odonata means "toothed" and refers to their sharp, pointed jaws. Dragonflies are large, slender insects. Their relatives, damselflies, are smaller and more delicate. Both dragonflies and damselflies come in many bright colors, including scarlet, blue and green.

Like bugs, they undergo incomplete metamorphosis, hatching as nymphs and gradually become more like adults. Both nymphs and adults are carnivores and expert hunters, but adults and young live in very different ways. Nymphs grow up underwater in ponds and streams. Adults are one of the largest winged insects and are powerful fliers.

▲ LARGE EYES

Dragonflies have extremely large compound eyes, as this close-up shows. The eyes cover most of the insect's head and almost meet at the top. Each compound eye has up to 30,000 lenses, each of which may help to build up a detailed picture. Dragonflies can detect movement easily and use their keen sight to track down their prey.

◄ FLYING CHAMP

Dragonflies are among the fastest insect fliers. They can race along at speeds of up to 60 miles per hour. Unlike other insects, their wings move independently. As each wing circles, it makes a figure eight. This helps the insect to accelerate, brake and hover in one place—and also to steer with great accuracy.

Dragonfly
(Trithemis annulata)

◄ ANCIENT INSECTS

Dragonflies are an ancient group of insects. From fossils, scientists have discovered that they flew on Earth 300 million years ago. They existed before the age of the dinosaurs. Some prehistoric dragonflies were giant insects, with wings that measured up to 2 feet across. No known modern species comes close to that size.

NIFTY HUNTER ►

A dragonfly feeds on a fly. It uses its sharp, pointed jaws to tear its prey into tiny chunks. Dragonflies often hunt in flight. They hold their spindly legs in front to form a small catching basket. Any flying insects within reach are quickly bagged. The dragonfly will sometimes even consume its prey in mid-flight.

◄ GROWING UP

Clinging to a plant stem, a young damselfly emerges from its final molt by a pond. Both dragonflies and damselflies lay their eggs in fresh water. The young hunt, feed and grow underwater. Gills on their abdomens allow them to extract oxygen from the water like fish. When fully grown, the nymph crawls up a plant stem and then molts for the last time. As its skin splits, the young adult climbs out.

DRYING OUT ►

A young dragonfly rests after emerging from its molted skin. Its short, crumpled wings and abdomen gradually lengthen and harden as blood is pumped into them. Its body colors will also appear soon. Adult dragonflies live only a few weeks, during which time they will mate and lay eggs.

Fleas, Grasshoppers and Mantids

▲ HIGH JUMP CHAMPION

With no wings, fleas cannot fly. They are, however, amazing leapers. A flea can jump 12 inches high—130 times its own height. If humans could leap as high as fleas, we would be able to jump over tall buildings! The incredible leaping ability of a flea allows it to hop on to much larger animals as they pass by.

Most beetles and bugs rely on the power of flight, but these three orders of insects have evolved different methods of moving around. Fleas are tiny, wingless parasites. Their strong muscles make them champion leapers. Fleas live on warm-blooded mammals and birds, and drink their blood. They belong to the order Siphonaptera, which refers to their sucking mouthparts and lack of wings.

Grasshoppers are also powerful leapers, well known for the loud, chirping noises they sing to attract a mate. These insects belong to the order Orthoptera, which means "straight wings." The grasshopper family includes crickets and locusts. Most grasshoppers are plant eaters.

Mantids belong to the order Dictyoptera, and all are carnivores. These large insects are disguised to blend in with their surroundings. This superb camouflage helps them catch their prey. Unlike grasshoppers and fleas, mantids are found mainly in warm countries.

DEADLY PEST ▶

A rat flea (right) feeds on human blood. Different species of fleas are designed to feed on certain types of animals. If hungry, however, a flea will suck any animal's blood. By feeding from various hosts (victims), fleas pass on diseases. In medieval times, they carried a terrible disease called bubonic plague. Known as the Black Death, it killed half the population of Europe. The fleas carried the disease after biting infected rats.

SPINY LEGS ▶

This close-up of a mantis shows the insect's spiny front legs. It uses its forelegs to capture insects, which it then eats alive. The mantis lurks among flowers or leaves, waiting for passing insects. When a victim gets close enough, the mantis lunges forward to grab its next meal.

Praying mantis
(*Mantis religiosa*)

Grasshopper
(Orthoptera)

◀ **ONE GIANT LEAP**

Grasshoppers escape from their enemies by leaping, as this one is doing. These insects have two pairs of wings but are not strong fliers. They can cover up to 3 feet in one single bound. Before it leaps, the grasshopper gathers its strong hind legs under its body. Muscles then pull on the upper and lower legs to straighten the limbs and hurl the insect into the air.

FLOWER DISGUISE ▶

Mantids use their camouflage to hunt down their prey. This beautiful tropical "flower" is actually a flower mantis. These amazing insects have flaps on their legs and heads that resemble the petals of flowers. Some mantids mimic green or dying leaves.

◀ **SINGING**

This male grasshopper is stridulating (singing) to attract a female. He produces a stream of high-pitched rasping sounds by rubbing his hind legs against his front wings. Crickets sing in a slightly different way—they rub rough patches on their wings together. These insects can detect sound through special "ears" on their legs or abdomens.

Beetles, Bugs and People

Beetles and bugs do many useful jobs that benefit people, either directly or indirectly. They fertilize plants and consume waste matter. They also provide a valuable food source for many other animals, including reptiles and birds.

However, most people regard many beetles and bugs as pests because they can harm us or our lands and possessions. Aphids, chafers and weevils attack orchards, vegetable plots and gardens. Woodboring beetles and carpet beetles damage timber, furniture, carpets and clothes. Blood-sucking bugs harm humans and livestock, and some carry dangerous diseases, such as malaria. People wage war against these pests – and many other harmless beetles and bugs. Some species are in danger of dying out altogether because people are killing them, or destroying the places in which they live.

▲ **CARPET-CRUNCHER**
A carpet beetle larva munches on a woolen carpet. These young beetles become pests when they hatch on carpets and clothes. The larvae have spines on their bodies that protect them from enemies. A close relative, the museum beetle, also causes havoc. It eats its way through preserved animal specimens in museums.

COLLECTING INSECTS ▶
If you are collecting insects, remember to handle them carefully so that you do not damage them. Always return insects to the place where you found them. Do not try to catch delicate insects such as dragonflies, or ones that could sting you, such as wasps.

Manna from Heaven
The Old Testament of the Bible tells how the ancient Israelites survived in the desert by eating "manna." After many centuries of debate, historians now believe this strange food may have been scale insects, living on tamarisk trees.

▲ **DUTCH ELM DISEASE**
Elm bark beetles (*Scolytus multistriatus*) are wood-borers. The fungus they carry causes Dutch elm disease, which kills elm trees. During the 1970s, a major outbreak of the disease destroyed most of the elm trees in the United States.

▲ **WOODWORM DAMAGE**
This chair has fallen prey to woodworm. These beetles (Anobiidae) can literally reduce wood to powder. Laid as eggs inside the timber, the young feed on the wood until they are ready to pupate. As winged adults, they quickly bore their way to freedom, leaving behind their telltale exit holes in the wood.

▲ **GARDENERS' FRIEND**
These black bean aphids (*Aphis fabae*) are infested with tiny parasitic wasps. The female wasp lays her eggs on the aphids. When the young hatch, they eat the bugs. Gardeners consider aphids a pest and welcome the wasps in their gardens. Wasps are sometimes used in large numbers by gardeners to control pests.

BUTTERFLIES AND MOTHS

Butterflies are the most beautiful of all insects, with big, vividly colored, triangular wings. On summer days, they can be seen fluttering slowly from flower to flower to sip nectar. Moths are a similar shape, but they are usually less brightly colored than butterflies. They also tend to fly mostly at night and rest by day, when their drab colors keep them hidden.

Winged Beauties

Butterflies and moths are the most beautiful of all insects. On sunny days, butterflies flit from flower to flower. Their slow, fluttering flight often reveals the full glory of their large, vividly colored wings. Moths are usually less brightly colored than butterflies and generally fly at night. Together, butterflies and moths make up one of the largest orders (groups) of insects, called Lepidoptera. This order includes more than 165,000 different species, of which 20,000 are types of butterfly and 145,000 are types of moth. The richest variety is found in tropical forests, but there are butterflies and moths in fields, woods, grasslands, deserts and mountains in every area of land in the world—except Antarctica.

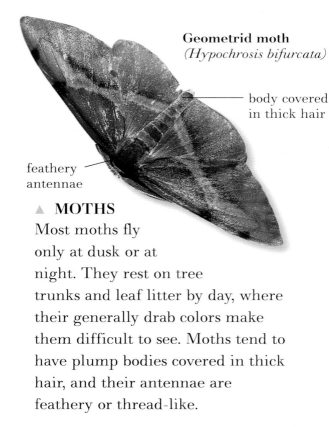

Geometrid moth
(Hypochrosis bifurcata)

body covered in thick hair

feathery antennae

▲ **MOTHS**
Most moths fly only at dusk or at night. They rest on tree trunks and leaf litter by day, where their generally drab colors make them difficult to see. Moths tend to have plump bodies covered in thick hair, and their antennae are feathery or thread-like.

▼ **RESTING BUTTERFLY**
You can usually tell a butterfly from a moth by the way it folds its wings when it is resting. A moth spreads its wings back like a tent, with only the upper sides visible. However, a butterfly settles with its wings folded flat with the uppersides together, so that only the undersides show.

Green-veined white butterfly
(Pieris napi)

Psyche and Aphrodite
The Ancient Greeks believed that, after death, their souls fluttered away from their bodies in the form of butterflies. The Greek symbol for the soul was a butterfly-winged girl called Psyche. According to legend, Aphrodite (goddess of love) was jealous of Psyche's beauty. She ordered her son Eros to make Psyche fall in love with him. Instead, Eros fell in love with her himself.

Blue morpho butterfly
(Morpho peleides)

antenna

compound eye
consists of up to
about 6,000
individual lenses

brightly colored
forewing

wing is
covered in
overlapping
scales

typical slim
body of a
butterfly

the hindwing
is smaller than
the forewing

tough outer coating
supports the body,
instead of an
internal skeleton

▲ FEATURES OF A BUTTERFLY

Butterflies tend to have brilliantly colored wings
and fly only during the day. They have slim bodies
without much hair, and their antennae are shaped
like clubs, with lumps at the ends. However, the
distinction between butterflies and moths is very
blurred, and some countries do not distinguish
between them at all.

▶ CATERPILLARS

A many-legged caterpillar hatches from
a butterfly's egg. When young, both
moths and butterflies are
caterpillars. Only
when they are big
enough do the
caterpillars go
through the
changes that
turn them into
winged adults.

Privet hawk moth caterpillar
(Sphinx ligustri)

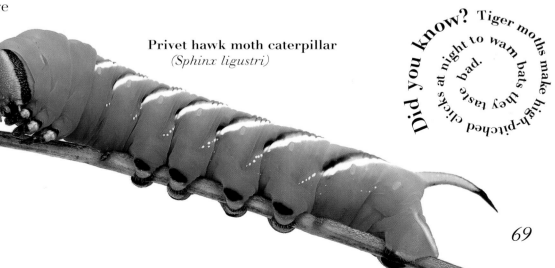

Did you know? Tiger moths make high-pitched clicks at night to warn bats they taste bad.

69

How Butterflies Look

a male Queen Alexandra's birdwing has brightly colored wings

Butterflies vary enormously in size and shape. In regions such as Europe and the United States they range from big butterflies such as the monarch, which has a wingspan of 4 inches, to the small blue, which is smaller than a postage stamp. The variation among tropical species is even greater. The largest butterfly in the world is the rare Queen Alexandra's birdwing. The female has a wingspan of 11 inches, which is more than 25 times the size of the minute Western pygmy blue. The shape of butterfly wings can be deceptive. In photographs and drawings, butterflies are usually shown with both pairs of wings stretched out fully. However, they are not always seen like this in nature. For example, sometimes the forewings may hide the hindwings.

Monarch butterfly
(Danaus plexippus)

◄ **MONARCH MIGRATIONS**
The monarch is one of the biggest butterflies outside of tropical regions. In North America it makes long journeys, called migrations, to spend the winter in warm areas such as California, Florida and Mexico. Some monarch butterflies fly from as far away as Canada.

▼ **COMMA BUTTERFLY**
Each species of butterfly has its own distinctive wing markings. The comma butterfly gets its name from the small, white C, or comma-shape, on the undersides of its hindwings.

Comma butterfly
(Polygonia c-album)

70

▼ BIG AS A BIRD

The Queen Alexandra's birdwing is a rare butterfly that lives only in the Northern Province of Papua New Guinea. Its wings are wider than those of many birds. Females can grow up to 11 inches.

Queen Alexandra's birdwing butterfly
(Ornithoptera alexandrae)

the bright yellow body warns predators that the butterfly is poisonous

Small blue butterfly
(Cupido minimus)

▲ SMALL BLUE

The small blue is the smallest butterfly in Great Britain. It is barely an inch across, even when fully grown. However, the tiny pygmy blue butterfly of North America is even smaller with a wingspan of between ½ and ¾ inch.

Peacock butterfly
(Inachis io)

▶ PEACOCK EYES

The peacock butterfly is easily identified by the pairs of markings on both the front and hindwings. These large spots look like eyes. It is one of the most common and distinctive butterflies in Europe and parts of Asia, including Japan.

Swallowtail butterfly
(Papilio machaon)

▶ A TAIL OF DECEPTION

The wing shapes of butterflies can vary dramatically from species to species. Many butterflies in the family called Papilionidae have distinctive tails on their wings, resembling swallows' tails. Some species of swallowtail use them to confuse predators. When the wings are folded, the tails look like antennae, so a predator may mistake the butterfly's tail-end for its head.

71

How Moths Look

American moon moth
(Actias luna)

Like butterflies, moths come in all shapes and sizes. There is also more variety in wing shape among moths than among butterflies. In terms of size, some of the smallest moth species have wingspans no wider than 3 millimeters. The biggest have wings that are almost as wide as this book, for example the Hercules moth of Australia and New Guinea and the bent-wing ghost moth of southeast Asia. The larvae (caterpillars) of small moths may be tiny enough to live inside seeds, fruits, stems, leaves and flowers. The caterpillars of larger moths are bigger, although some do live inside tree trunks and stems.

▲ MOON MOTH

The American moon moth shows just how delicate and attractive large moths can be. Its wingspan is about 12 inches. and it has long, slender tails on its hindwings. When it is resting on a tree, its body and head are so well hidden by its big wings that any predatory bird will peck harmlessly at its tails. This allows the moth time to escape.

Garden tiger moth
(Arctia caja)

▼ ELEPHANT HAWK MOTH

Many moths are less colorful than butterflies, but they are not all drably colored. For example, the elephant hawk moth is a beautiful insect with delicate pink wings that blend in well with its favorite flowers (valerian and pink honeysuckle). However, the elephant hawk moth flies at night, so it is not often seen in its full glory.

◀ COLOR RANGE

Identifying moths can be quite difficult, as some species show a wide range of coloring. For example, many garden tiger moths are slightly different colors from each other. As a result of this variety, scientists often use the garden tiger moth for breeding experiments.

Elephant hawk moth *(Deilephila elpenor)*

72

▶ INDIAN MOTH

This moth belongs to the family Pyralidae and comes from southern India. This tiny moth has a wingspan of just ¾ inch. The distinctive white bands on its wings break up the moth's outline and make it more difficult to spot when at rest.

Lepyrodes neptis

Did you know? The Big Beet Borer moth (*Melitia gloriosa*) has a furry striped abdomen and looks like a bee.

▼ WIDE WINGS

The giant Atlas moth of India and southeast Asia is one of the world's largest moths. Only the giant Agrippa moth of South America has wider wings, with a span of up to 12 inches. Some Atlas moths grow almost as big as this entire double page when their wings are opened fully. They have shiny triangles on their wings that are thought to confuse predators by reflecting light.

Giant atlas moth
(Archaeoattacus edwardsi)

▲ MANY PLUME MOTH

The beautiful feathery wings of this unusual looking moth give it its name, the many plume moth (*Alucita hexadactyla*). Each of its fore and hindwings is split into six slender feathery sections, or plumes.

▼ LARGE CATERPILLAR

Caterpillars have many different shapes and sizes, just like moths. The young acacia emperor moth is one of the biggest caterpillars. Although they are generally sausage-shaped, some caterpillars are twig-like, making them hard to see in a bush or tree.

73

Body Parts

In many ways, butterflies and moths are similar to other insects. Their bodies are divided into three parts—the head, the thorax and the abdomen. The mouth, eyes and antennae (feelers) are situated on the head. The thorax is the body's powerhouse, driving the legs and wings. The abdomen is where food is digested. Like all insects, butterflies and moths have bodies, which are covered by a tough outer shell, called an exoskeleton. However, butterflies and moths also have unique features, such as their big, flat wings and long proboscises (tongues).

abdomen

▲ **EGG CENTER**
The abdomen (rear section) houses a butterfly's digestive system. It also produces eggs in female butterflies and moths and sperm in males.

◄ **SWEET SUCKING**
This butterfly is feeding on a prickly pear cactus fruit in Mexico. Butterflies and moths feed mainly on nectar and other sweet juices. They suck them up through long tube-like tongues called proboscises. Butterflies and moths have no jaws.

▲ **FEEDING STRAW**
A purple emperor butterfly rolls out its proboscis to feed. The proboscis stretches out almost as long as its body. When a butterfly rests, it rolls up its long proboscis beneath its head. Hawk moths have the longest proboscises.

▶ **CONNECTED WINGS**
The forewings and hindwings of most moths overlap. Although each pair of wings is separate, they act together because long bristles on the hindwing catch onto hooks on the underside of the forewing, something like a door latch.

burnet moth with wings raised, showing the bristle linking the forewing and hindwing

► **MOTH WINGS**

Butterflies and moths each have two pairs of large, flat wings and three pairs of legs. The wings and legs are attached to the thorax (the mid-section of the body). The two pairs of wings are not always visible.

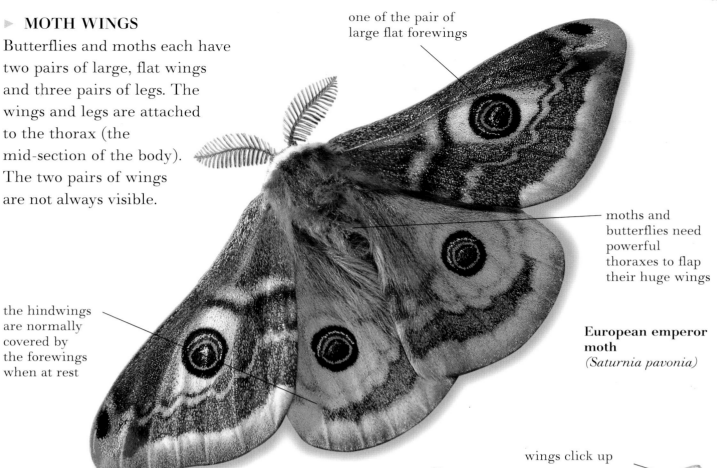

one of the pair of large flat forewings

moths and butterflies need powerful thoraxes to flap their huge wings

European emperor moth
(Saturnia pavonia)

the hindwings are normally covered by the forewings when at rest

▲ **SENSITIVE FEET**

Moths and butterflies taste with their tarsi (feet). When they land on a flower, they will not unroll their tongues to feed unless their feet sense the sweetness of nectar. Females stamp their tarsi on leaves to decide if they are ripe for egg-laying. They will lay eggs only if the leaves release the correct scents.

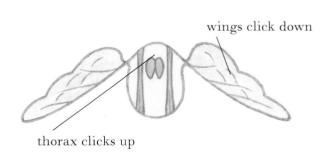

wings click up

thorax clicks down

wings click down

thorax clicks up

▲ **FLIGHT**

The wings are joined to the thorax (mid-section). Muscles pull the top of the thorax down, making the wings flip up. Then the muscles pull the thorax in, making it thinner so the top clicks back up again, flipping the wings down.

75

European map butterfly
(*Araschnia levana*)

Scaly Wings

The scientific name for butterflies and moths, Lepidoptera, refers to the minute scales covering their wings. *Lepis* is the Ancient Greek word for scale, and *pteron* means wing. The scales are actually flattened hairs and each one is connected to the wings by a short stalk. These delicate scales give butterfly wings their amazing colors, but can rub off easily like dust. Underneath the scales, butterfly and moth wings are transparent like the wings of other insects. The vivid colors of the scales come either from pigments (colored chemicals) in the scales or the way their structure reflects light.

▲ SCENTED SCALES

Many male butterflies have special scales called *androconia* that help them to attract mates. These scales scent the wings with an odor that stimulates females.

▲ OVERLAPPING SCALES

Tiny scales overlap and completely coat the wings. They are so loosely attached that they often shake off in flight.

▲ CELL SPACE

The areas between the wing veins are called cells. All the cells radiate outward from one vein at the base of the wings.

**Black-veined
white butterfly**
(*Aporia crataegi*)

▼ WING VEINS

Butterfly and moth wings are supported by a framework of veins. These veins are filled with air, nerve fibers and blood. The pattern of the veins helps to classify butterflies and moths into a number of families.

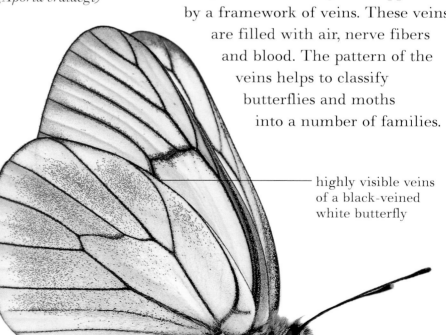

highly visible veins
of a black-veined
white butterfly

▶ SCALING DOWN

A large white butterfly takes off from a buttercup. Butterflies in flight naturally lose scales from time to time. The loss does not seem to harm some species. However, others find themselves unable to fly without a reasonable coating of scales to soak up the sun and warm their bodies.

Did you know? The wings of the glasswing butterfly are transparent, making it almost invisible.

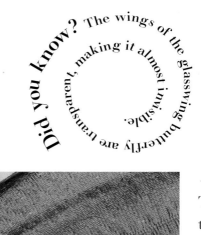

◀ MORPHO WING

The metallic blue wings of the South American morpho butterfly shimmer in the sunlight. This effect is produced by the special way the surface texture of their wings reflects light. When filmed by a video camera that is sensitive to invisible ultraviolet light, these scales flash like a beacon.

Butterfly Ball
The butterfly's fragile beauty has always inspired artists. In the 1800s, many European artists portrayed them as fairies, with human bodies and butterfly wings.

▶ EYE TO EYE

The patterns of scales on some butterflies form circles that resemble the bold, staring eyes of larger animals. Scientists think that these eyespots may have developed to startle and scare away predators such as birds. However, the eyespots on other butterflies may be used to attract mates.

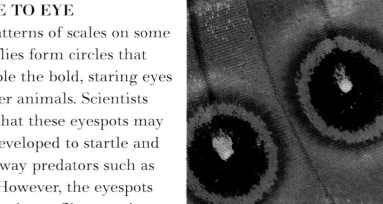

SUN LOVERS

Butterflies and moths can only fly if their body temperature reaches at least 75–85°F. If they are too cold, the muscles powering the wings do not work. To warm up, butterflies bask in the sun, so that the wing scales soak up sunlight like solar panels. Night-flying moths shiver their wings to warm them instead.

Butterflies and moths fly in a different way from other insects. They fly similarly to birds. Most insects simply beat their wings very rapidly to move through the air. Since they can only stay aloft if they beat their wings fast enough, they soon run out of energy. However, many butterflies ripple their wings slowly up and down. Some, such as the white admiral, can even glide on currents of air with just an occasional flap to keep them aloft. This enables them to fly amazing distances. Flight patterns vary from the fluttering of the wood white to the soaring of the purple emperor butterflies. Wingbeat tends to be faster in the smaller species, with the skipper family having the fastest wingbeat of all. Moths, such as the hawk moths with their jet plane-like wings, fly at fast speeds in a generally straight line.

TWISTERS

To the human eye, the wings of butterflies and moths appear simply to flap. However, freeze-frame photography reveals that the bases of the wings twist as they move up and down, so that the wing tips move in a figure eight.

Butterflies look like clumsy fliers, but their acrobatic twists and turns enable them to escape sparrows and other predatory birds. Some moths can fly at up to 30 miles per hour when frightened.

Flight

the wings push air backward

the butterfly is propelled forward

a butterfly lifts its wings upward

as the wings come down again, they provide lift to keep the butterfly up

UP, UP AND AWAY

The wings are stiff along the front edges and at the bases, but the rest of the wing is flexible. The stiff front edges of the wing give the butterfly lift, like the wings of an aircraft, as it flies forward. The flexing of the rest of the wing pushes air backward and drives the butterfly forward.

GRACEFUL GLIDERS

Butterflies in the family Nymphalidae, such as this Painted Lady (*Vanessa cardui*), tend to flap their wings only occasionally when in flight. They prefer to glide gracefully from flower to flower, with just the odd beat of their wings.

Senses

Butterflies and moths have a very different range of senses from humans. Instead of having just two eyes, they have compound eyes made up of hundreds or even thousands of tiny lenses. They also have incredibly sensitive antennae (feelers) which they use not only to smell food, but also to hear and feel things. The antennae play a vital part in finding a mate and deciding where to lay eggs. They may even detect taste and temperature change. Butterflies and moths have a good sense of taste and smell in their tarsi (feet), too. Moths hear sounds with a form of ears called tympanal organs. These little membranes are situated on the thorax or abdomen and vibrate like a drum when sound hits them.

▲ **ANTENNAE**
The feathery side branches on an Atlas moth's antennae increase the surface area for detecting scent, like the spikes on a TV aerial. They allow the male moth to pinpoint certain smells, such as the scent of a potential mate, at huge distances.

▲ **SMELL THE WIND**
A butterfly's antennae act like an external nose packed with highly sensitive smell receptors. They can pick up minute traces of chemicals in the air that are undetectable to the human nose.

◄ **ATTRACTIVE ANTENNAE**
Male longhorn moths (*Adelidae*) have very long antennae. These antennae are used to pick up scent, but they also have another, very different, job. They shine in the sunlight and attract females when the males dance up and down in the afternoon.

80

moth's
head

▲ HEARING BODY

Many moths have "ears"
made up of tiny
membranes stretched
over little cavities. These
ears are situated on the
thorax. When the
membranes are vibrated
by a sound, a nerve sends
a signal to the brain.
These ears are highly
sensitive to the high-
pitched sounds of bats,
which prey on moths.

a noctuid moth
showing the
position of the
ears at the rear of
the thorax

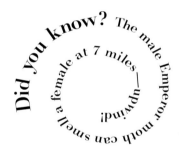

Did you know? The male Emperor moth can smell a female at 7 miles—upwind!

◀ MULTI-VISION

The compound eyes of an
orange-tip butterfly are
large. The thousands of
lenses in a compound eye
each form their own
picture of the world.
The butterfly's brain puts
the images together into
one picture. Although
butterflies are quite
nearsighted, they can
see all around using their
multiple eyes.

▼ FEELING FOR FLOWERS

Butterflies and moths find the flowers they
want to feed on mainly
by the incredibly
sensitive sense
of smell their
antennae give
them. This
enables them
to pick up the
scent of a single
bloom from some
distance away.

▼ A CASE OF THE BLUES

Butterflies don't see flowers such as this evening
primrose the way we do,
for their eyes are
not very senstive
to red and
yellow light.
But they can
see ultraviolet
light, which we
cannot see. They
see flowers in the
colors shown here.

Eggs

Butterflies and moths begin life as tiny eggs. After mating, some females simply scatter their eggs as they fly. However, most females seek a suitable place to lay their eggs, either individually or in batches of up to 1,000 or more. The leaves or stems of particular plants are common sites as they will provide food for the caterpillars after hatching. A female butterfly uses her sensitive antennae to locate the correct plant species. She stamps or scratches the leaves with her feet to check that the scent is right and that no other butterfly has laid eggs there before. Once she has laid her eggs, the female flies off almost immediately.

eggs emerge through the ovipositor

Large white butterfly
(Pieris brassicae)

▲ **EGG OOZE**
A female butterfly pushes her eggs out, one by one, through her ovipositor (the egg-laying duct at the end of her abdomen). The eggs ooze out in a kind of glue that sticks them in place as it hardens.

a Peacock butterfly's eggs, laid on the underside of a nettle leaf

▲ **RIDGED EGG**
The egg of the painted lady butterfly has a glassy shell with elaborate ridges. The shape of the egg is fairly constant in each family.

▲ **EGG SITE**
A peacock butterfly has laid her eggs on a sheltered part of the plant. This will provide them with warmth and protection, as well as food. Many butterflies and moths lay their eggs in random patterns, which improves the chances of predatory insects missing some of them.

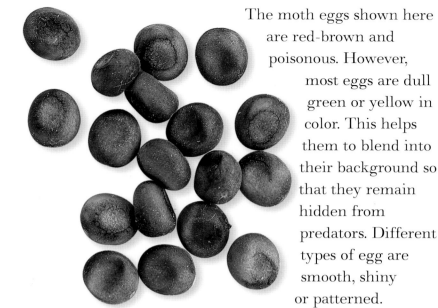

▼ EGGS IN CLOSE-UP

The moth eggs shown here are red-brown and poisonous. However, most eggs are dull green or yellow in color. This helps them to blend into their background so that they remain hidden from predators. Different types of egg are smooth, shiny or patterned.

▲ DIFFERENT NESTS

Some moths lay their eggs along a grass stem, so they look like the stem itself. Others lay eggs in dangling strings or in overlapping rows like tiles on a roof.

◄ EGG SHAPES

The eggs of a large white butterfly are diamond-shaped. Butterfly eggs vary in shape from the spiny balls of the white admiral to the cones of the silver-spotted skipper. All have a hard shell lined on the inside with wax, which protects the developing caterpillar inside.

► HATCHING EGGS

Most butterfly eggs hatch within a few days of being laid. However, a few types of egg pass an entire winter before hatching. They hatch when temperatures begin to rise and the caterpillars stand a chance of survival. The eggs grow darker in color just before hatching. The tiny caterpillars bite their way out from their shells. Their minute jaws cut a circle in the shell that is just big enough for the head to squeeze through.

newly hatched caterpillars of the large white butterfly

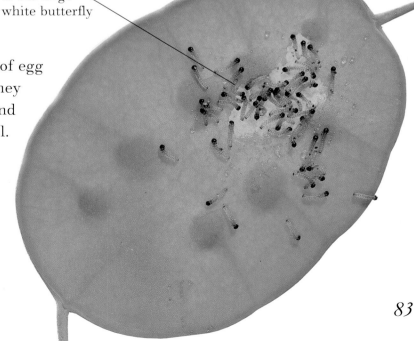

The Caterpillar

Once a caterpillar (or larva) bites its way from the egg, it immediately begins eating. While most adult butterflies and moths survive on nectar, a caterpillar chomps its way through leaves, fruits and stems. It grows rapidly, shedding its skin several times as it swells. Within a month, it may be fully grown and ready to change into a butterfly or moth. Caterpillars are far more numerous than adult butterflies and moths but most are eaten by predators or killed by diseases. They hide among vegetation and crevices in bark, often feeding at night to avoid danger.

Five-spotted hawk moth caterpillar
(*Manduca quinquemaculatus*)

head

true legs

thorax

Abdomen

spine or horn at the tip of the abdomen

each proleg ends in a ring of crochets (hooks) that hold onto stems and leaves

anal proleg or clasper enables a caterpillar to cling to plants

◄ **CATERPILLAR PARTS**

Caterpillars have big heads with strong jaws for snipping off food. Their long, soft bodies are divided into thirteen segments. The front segments become the thorax in the adult insect, and the rear segments become the abdomen.

PROLEGS ►

The caterpillar of an emperor gum moth (*Antheraea eucalypti*) has five pairs of prolegs (false legs) on its abdomen. All caterpillars have these prolegs, which they lose as adults. Caterpillars also have three pairs of true legs, which become the legs of the adult.

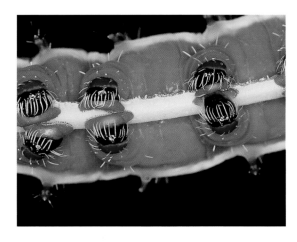

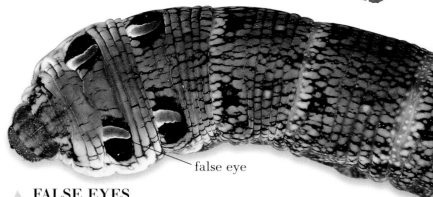

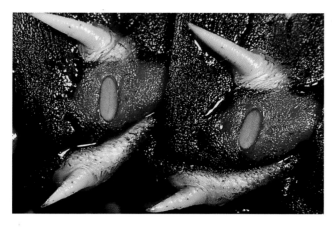

▲ **BREATHING HOLES**

A caterpillar does not have lungs for breathing like humans. Instead, it has tiny holes called spiracles that draw oxygen into the body tissues. There are several spiracles on both sides of the caterpillar.

false eye

▲ **FALSE EYES**

The large eye shapes behind the head of an elephant hawk moth caterpillar are actually false eyes for scaring predators. In fact, caterpillars can barely see at all. They possess six small eyes that can only distinguish between dark and light.

Did you know? Caterpillars can close up their spiracles and survive underwater for hours.

◄ **CHANGING SKIN**

Every week or so, the skin of a growing caterpillar grows too tight. It then splits down the back to reveal a new skin underneath. At first the new skin is soft and stretchy. As the caterpillar sheds its old skin, it swells the new one by taking in air through its spiracles (air holes). It then lies still for a few hours while the new skin hardens.

◄ **FLY ATTACK**

A puss moth caterpillar can defend itself against predators. It puffs up its front and whips its tail like a tiny dragon, before spraying a jet of poison over its foe.

SILK MAKERS ►

Peacock butterfly caterpillars live and feed in web-like tents. They spin these tents from silken thread. All caterpillars can produce this sticky liquid from the spinnerets under their mouths. The silk helps them to hold onto surfaces as they move around.

Hungry Caterpillars

tunnel left by leaf-mining caterpillar

▲ LEAF MINING

Many tiny caterpillars eat their way through the inside of the leaf instead of crawling across the surface. This activity is known as leaf mining. Often, their progress is revealed by a pale tunnel beneath the leaf surface.

Caterpillars are incredible eating machines, munching their way through several times their own body weight of food in a single day. This is why they grow so rapidly. Their first meal is usually the egg from which they hatch. Once that is gone, they move on to the nearest food source. Some eat nearby unhatched eggs, and a few even eat other caterpillars. Most feed on the leaves and stems of their own particular food plant. This is usually the plant on which they hatched. However, some moth caterpillars eat wool or cotton. The food is stored in the caterpillar's body and is used for growth and energy in the later stages of its development. The caterpillar stage lasts for at least two weeks, and sometimes much longer.

sensitive palps are located near the mouth

the true legs are used to grip foliage

Swallowtail butterfly caterpillar
(Papilio machaon)

▲ FEEDING HABITS

Caterpillars eat different food plants from those used by the adults. Swallowtail butterfly caterpillars feed on fennel, carrots and milk-parsley. Adult swallowtail butterflies drink the nectar of thistles and buddleias.

▶ IDENTIFYING FOOD

The head end of a privet hawk moth caterpillar is shown in close-up here. A caterpillar probably identifies food using sensitive organs called palps that are just in front of the mouth.

◄ FAST EATERS

Cabbages are the main food plants of the large white butterfly caterpillar. These insects can strip a field of foliage in a few nights. This is why many farmers and gardeners kill caterpillars with pesticides. However, their numbers may be controlled naturally by parasitic wasps, as long as the wasps are not killed by pesticides.

Alice in Wonderland

In Lewis Carroll's magical book Alice in Wonderland, *a hookah-smoking caterpillar discusses with Alice what it is like to change size. Carroll was probably thinking of how caterpillars grow in stages.*

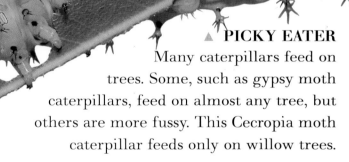

▲ PICKY EATER

Many caterpillars feed on trees. Some, such as gypsy moth caterpillars, feed on almost any tree, but others are more fussy. This Cecropia moth caterpillar feeds only on willow trees.

▲ PROCESSIONARY CATERPILLARS

The caterpillars of processionary moths travel to feeding areas in a neat row. They also rest together in silken nests. These insects are poisonous and so do not try to hide as others do.

Focus on

Moth caterpillars ooze out a silky liquid thread from ducts called spinnerets. One species produces a liquid so strong and fine that it can be used in silk, one of the most beautiful and luxurious of all fabrics. This caterpillar, that of the *Bombyx mori* moth, is known as the silkworm. In China, it has been cultivated for its silk for almost 5,000 years. According to legend, in about 2,700 B.C. the Chinese princess Si-Ling-Chi first discovered how to use the silk worm's cocoon to make silk thread. She was known thereafter as *Seine-Than* (the Silk Goddess).

1 The silkworm, (*Bombyx mori*), feeds entirely on the leaves of just one plant, the mulberry tree. Today, silkworms do not live in the wild. They are farmed and fed on chopped mulberry leaves.

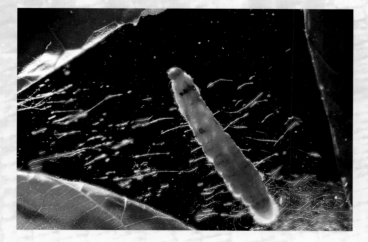

2 When the silkworm is ready to change into an adult moth, it finds a suitable spot between the mulberry leaves. Once settled, it begins to ooze silk thread from its spinneret.

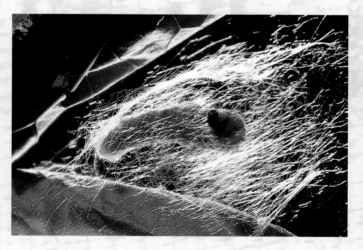

3 At first, the silk forms just a flimsy curtain, with only a few threads strung between the leaves. The silkworm is still clearly visible at this stage.

Making Silk

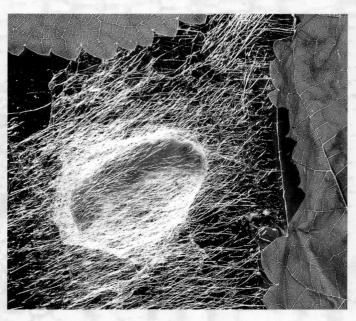

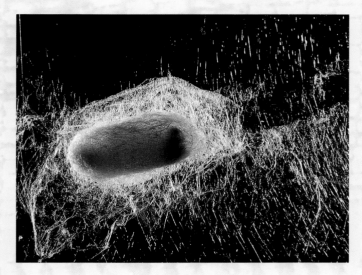

5 Inside the cocoon, the silkworm becomes a pupa (also known as a chrysalis). This is a stage in the development of moths and butterflies when they neither feed nor move. They emerge from this stage as adult insects.

4 After a few hours the silkworm stops running the silk between the leaves and begins to wrap it around itself. It uses about half a mile of silk to completely encase itself in a cocoon of the gummy thread.

6 Only a few pupae are allowed to emerge as adult *Bombyx mori* moths for breeding. Most cocoons are plunged into boiling water, which kills the pupa and dissolves the gum on the silk. The fine silk from several cocoons is twisted together to make usable silk thread.

Pupae

After about a month of eating and growing, a caterpillar is ready to pupate (become a pupa). This is when it transforms into an adult butterfly or moth. Pupae are defenseless, so many moth caterpillars spin a silken cocoon around themselves for protection. Many others tunnel into the ground before pupating. Most butterfly pupae are naked, but they are generally well camouflaged or hidden in leaf litter. A cocoon looks lifeless, but inside there is continuous activity as the caterpillar gradually transforms itself. This process, called metamorphosis, can take just a few days, although in some species it may be over a year before the adult insect finally emerges.

caterpillar of Large Tortoiseshell butterfly shedding its skin as it becomes a pupa

◀ **HANGING ON**
Many butterfly caterpillars stick themselves onto branches and stems with a pad of silk before pupating. Then they shed their old skin without dropping to the ground. Other caterpillars bury themselves in the soil or leaf litter.

▲ **HIBERNATING PUPA**
Some pupae, such as this brown hairstreak butterfly, complete their development in a couple of weeks. Other species pass the winter in a state of suspended development called diapause. This is very common among temperate butterflies and moths.

▶ **UP OR DOWN**
The pupae of white and swallowtail butterflies stick upward, held in place by a silk thread around the middle. These are called succinct pupae. Other pupae hang head-down from branches. They are called suspended pupae.

pupa sticking upward, held in place by a silk thread

elephant hawk moth pupa with wing veins visible through the surface

old skin shed during the caterpillar's transformation into a pupa

◄ DEVELOPING PUPA

The outlines of the wings, legs and antennae are faintly visible on the surface of the pupa, showing that it is almost ready to hatch.. Inside, the tissues that made up the caterpillar's body dissolve, ready for rebuilding as an adult.

FAILED PROTECTION ►

The pupa of this emperor moth (*Saturnia pavonia*) has been eaten away from the inside by the larva of a parasitic fly. The cocoon has been cut away to reveal the hole from which the fly grub has emerged. Pupae are never completely safe from predators.

hole in moth pupa

pupa of parasite

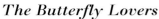

The Butterfly Lovers
An old Chinese tale tells of Zhu Yingtai, who disguises herself as a boy to go to college. There, she falls in love with Liang Shanbo. But Liang is unaware she is a girl, and Zhu is forced to marry a rich man's son. Liang realizes his mistake and dies broken-hearted. When Zhu hears, she takes her life in despair. The gods take pity and the pair are reunited as butterflies.

Did you know? *Some pupae resemble dead leaves or even bird droppings to trick predators.*

moth just hatched from pupa in cocoon

► EMERGING ADULT

Butterfly pupae vary considerably in color and shape. Some fritillary butterfly pupae have shiny patches that look like raindrops, but most moth pupae are brown or black bullet-shaped objects. Even experts find it difficult to determine the species to which they belong. Only when all the changes are complete and the moth emerges as an imago (adult) does the identity of the insect become clear.

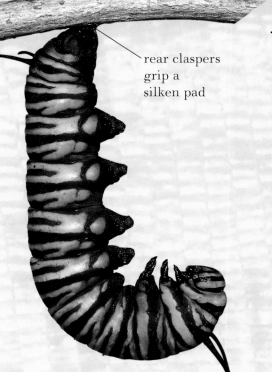

rear claspers grip a silken pad

Focus on

Pupation (changing from a caterpillar to a butterfly or moth) is one of the most astonishing transformations undergone by any living creature. Inside the chrysalis, or pupa, the body parts of the caterpillar gradually dissolve. New features grow in their place, including a totally different head and body, and two pairs of wings. This whole process can take less than a week. When these changes are complete, a fully-formed imago (adult moth or butterfly) emerges almost magically from the nondescript pouch.

1 The monarch butterfly caterpillar (*Danaus plexippus*) spins a silken pad on a plant stem and grips it firmly with its rear claspers. It then sheds its skin to reveal the chrysalis, which clings to the silken pad with tiny hooks.

2 The chrysalis of the monarch is plump, pale and studded with golden spots. It appears lifeless except for the occasional twitch. However, changes can sometimes barely be seen through the skin.

fully formed chrysalis

chrysalis darkens before opening

3 The chrysalis grows dark just before the adult emerges. The wing pattern becomes visible through the skin. The butterfly then pumps body fluids to its head and thorax. Next, the chrysalis cracks open behind the head and along the front of the wing.

Metamorphosis

4 The butterfly swallows air to make itself swell up, which splits the chrysalis even more. The insect emerges shakily and hangs down, clinging tightly to the chrysalis skin.

5 The newly emerged adult slowly pumps blood into the veins in its wings, which begin to straighten out. The insect hangs down with its head up so that the force of gravity helps to stretch the wings. After about half an hour, it reaches its full size.

split skin of chrysalis

wing veins with blood pumping into them

wings are soft and crumpled

6 The butterfly basks in the sun for an hour or two while its wings dry out and harden. After a few trial flaps of its wings, it is ready to fly away and begin its life as an adult butterfly.

the adult butterfly tests its wings before its maiden flight

Finding a Mate

Common blue butterfly
(Polyommatus icarus)

A butterfly's life is usually very short, so it has only a little while to find a mate. Most females live for just a few days, so they must begin to lay eggs as soon as possible. Male butterflies emerge from their pupae a little earlier than the females. This allows some males to mate with a newly emerged female while her wings are still soft and crumpled. However, most males court their female with elaborate flights and dances. Males and females are drawn to each other by the shape of each other's wings and by the colorful and striking patterns on them. The males also spread powerful scents that stimulate females to approach them and land alongside. Then they circle each other, performing complicated courtship dances.

▲ **COURTING BLUES**
When courting a female, a male butterfly often flutters its wings flamboyantly. It looks as if it is showing off, but it is really wafting its pheromones (the scents from special scales on its forewings). Only if the female picks up these pheromones with her antennae will she be willing to mate.

Did you know? People with sensitive noses say the pheromones of the wall brown butterfly smell like chocolate.

◀ **LARGE COPPER PAIR**
This pair of butterflies is about to mate. When she is ready, the female will fly away and land with her wings half open. The male will flutter down on top of her and begin to caress her abdomen with his rear end. The male then turns around to face the opposite way as they mate. The pair may remain joined like this for hours.

Madame Butterfly

One of the most famous operas is Puccini's Madame Butterfly, *written in 1904. The opera is set in the 1800s in Osaka, Japan. It tells the story of an American officer, James Pinkerton, who falls in love with a beautiful young Japanese girl. His nickname for her is Butterfly. They have a child, but Pinkerton abandons Butterfly for his wife in America. The opera ends as Butterfly dies broken-hearted.*

▼ SCENT POWER

A butterfly's scent plays a major role in attracting a mate. The scents come from glands on the abdomen of a female. On a male, the scents come from special wing scales called androconia. A male often rubs his wings over the female's antennae.

androconia scales release scent

▼ MALE AND FEMALE

Often, female butterflies are drab, while males are brightly colored. The male orange-tip, for example, has a distinctive bright orange colored tip to its wings. However, the ends of the female orange-tip's wings (see top right of page) are gray-black.

Male orange-tip butterfly (*Anthocharis cardamines*)

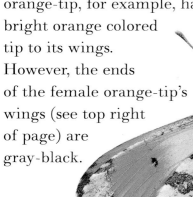

▼ SINGLE MATE

Male butterflies mate several times in their lifetime. However a female butterfly usually mates just once and then concentrates on egg-laying. Once they have mated, many females release a special pheromone that deters other males.

Female orange-tip butterfly (*Anthocharis cardamines*)

▲ FLYING TOGETHER

Butterflies usually stay on the ground or on a plant while coupling. But if danger threatens, they can fly off linked together, with one (called the carrier) pulling the other backward.

Flower Power

Butterflies and moths have a close relationship with plants, especially with those that flower. Many live much of their lives on a particular kind of vegetation. They begin life as eggs on the plant, feed on it while they are caterpillars and change into a pupa while attached to it. Finally, the adult may sip the nectar from its blooms. Just as butterflies rely on flowers for food, many flowers rely on visiting butterflies to spread their pollen. The bright colors and attractive scents of flowers may have evolved to attract butterflies and other insects such as bees. When a butterfly lands on a flower to drink nectar, grains of pollen cling to its body. Some of the pollen grains rub off on the next flower the butterfly visits.

▲ FEEDING ON FUCHSIA

The caterpillar of the elephant hawk moth feeds on the leaves of fuchsias. Many lepidopterists (butterfly and moth experts) grow fuchsias in their gardens for the pleasure of seeing this spectacular caterpillar. However, some gardeners think of the moths as pests for the same reason.

▼ THISTLE LOVER

A brimstone butterfly (*Gonepteryx rhamni*) settles on a thistle to feed. It is common throughout Europe in light woodland areas and in the open countryside at heights of up to 6,500 feet. The brimstone also likes to feed on a wide range of garden flowers.

▲ FABULOUS FUCHSIAS

The small elephant hawk moth is shown here drinking nectar from a fuchsia. Rather than settling on a flower, these large, powerful moths often feed while hovering in front of them.

▶ FEEDING TOGETHER

A group of small tortoiseshell butterflies (*Aglais urticae*) is shown here sipping nectar together. Small tortoiseshells are widespread throughout Europe. They are attracted to a wide range of blooms including buddleia, Michaelmas daisy and sedum that are found in fields, by roadsides and in yards.

◀ STINGING NETTLES

The adult peacock butterfly (*Inachis io*) sits on a weed called the stinging nettle. It generally feeds on flowers such as buddleia. However, the caterpillars of this species feed almost exclusively on nettles. Many gardeners clear away this unattractive weed, which causes peacock butterflies to lay their eggs elsewhere.

Did you know? Buddleia is so attractive to many butterflies that it is sometimes called the butterfly bush.

▼ GOURMET FOOD

This beautiful red spotted purple swallowtail butterfly feeds on a desert flower in Arizona. Butterflies and moths are adapted to the specific environment in which they live. Swallowtails are common throughout Europe, but there they sip nectar from meadow and orchard flowers.

Red spotted purple swallowtail butterfly
(*Basilarchia astyanax*)

97

Nectar and Food

Butterflies and moths cannot chew food. Instead, they suck up liquids through their long proboscises (tongues), which act like drinking straws. Their preferred food is nectar. This sugary fluid is produced in the nectaries of flowers in order to attract insects such as butterflies and bees. Most species of butterfly survive on nectar alone and spend most of their brief lives flitting from flower to flower in search of this juice. Some woodland species extract sweet liquids from a wide variety of sources, including rotting fruit and sap oozing from wounds in trees. A few species even suck on dung. However, these sources do not provide much real sustenance, which is why butterflies rarely live for more than a few days.

Postman butterfly
(*Heliconius*)

▲ LONG LIFE

Heliconius butterflies of the tropical forests of South America are among the few relatively long-lived butterflies. They are able to live for 130 days or more, compared with barely 20 for most temperate species. *Heliconius* butterflies feed on passion fruit flowers.

▲ FRUIT EATERS

The first generation of comma butterflies appears each year in early summer. These insects feed on the delicate white blossoms of blackberries, because the fruit has not yet ripened at this time. The second generation appears in autumn and feeds on the ripe blackberries.

Red admiral butterfly
(*Vanessa atalanta*)

▼ CIDER DRINKING

In autumn, butterflies such as the red admiral and the Camberwell beauty often feed on rotting fruit. Sometimes the juice has fermented to alcohol, and the red admiral may be seen reeling around as if drunk.

◄ DRINKING STRAW

Many flowers hide their nectaries deep inside the flowers in order to draw the butterfly right onto their pollen sacs. Many butterflies have developed very long proboscises to reach the nectar. They probe deep into the flowers to suck up the juice.

▲ HOVERING HAWK MOTHS

The day-flying hummingbird hawk moth gets its name from its habit of hovering in front of flowers like a hummingbird as it sips nectar, rather than landing on the flower. Moths from the hawk moth family have the longest proboscises of all. One member, known as Darwin's hawk moth, has a proboscis that reaches to between 12 and 14 inches—about three times the length of its body.

► WOODLAND VARIETY

Many woodland butterflies extract juice from a variety of sources. The speckled wood butterfly sometimes sips nectar from bluebells. However, it feeds mainly on honeydew. This is the sugary secretion of tiny insects called aphids. The leaves of flowers are often coated with honeydew.

Speckled wood butterfly
(Pararge aegeria)

▲ NIGHT FEEDER

Noctuid moths often sip nectar from ragworts in meadows by moonlight. In temperate countries, these moths mostly feed on warm summer nights. They get their name from the Latin word *noctuis*, which means night.

At Ground Level

Butterflies need warmth in order to fly. In tropical regions it is usually warm enough for butterflies to fly for most of the day. But in cooler countries, they often spend much of the day resting. They spread out their wings and turn with the sun to soak up the rays. Male butterflies and moths also gather at muddy puddles or on damp earth to drink. This activity is known as puddling. At dusk, most butterflies seek a safe place to roost (rest) for the night. Moths generally hide during the day. They conceal themselves against tree bark or under leaves so they cannot be seen by predators.

▲ **LAZY DAYS**

A day's undisturbed rest is important for night-flying moths such as this Sussex emerald. It rests on or under leaves with its green wings outstretched, well disguised among the vegetation. Most other geometer moths rest in this position during the day, on leaves or against tree bark. Before flight, they shiver to warm up their wings.

▲ **DRY PUDDLING**

A Malayan butterfly sucks up mineral-rich water from sand through its proboscis (tongue). Some species of butterfly do not need a puddle in order to go puddling. In some dry regions, the male butterfly may be able to get the sodium it needs by spitting on and sucking dry stones, gravel or even the dried carcasses of animals.

▲ **SALT SEEKERS**

Puddling is a common activity in warm regions. However it is not always a communal activity. In some regions butterflies and moths puddle on their own. Although they appear to be drinking, only males seem to puddle like this. It is believed that they absorb important salts dissolved in the water. Sodium is needed to produce the sperm packets passed on to females during mating.

▶ BASKING ON LICHEN

A small tortoiseshell butterfly (*Aglais urticae*) basks in a park on a carpet of lichen. It rests with its wings open wide and flat, to soak up the sun's warmth. The small tortoiseshell lives in cooler parts of the world, in Europe, Siberia and Japan. It therefore needs to bask in the sunshine to warm up its wing muscles before flight.

Did you know? The grayling butterfly tilts to one side while resting to reduce the shadow cast by its wings.

▲ SUN LOVERS

The marbled white butterfly and other members of the Satyridae family have an unusual way of holding their wings when basking. They are held in a V-shape instead of fully opened or folded upright. The white of their wings reflects sunlight onto their abdomens.

Black-veined white butterfly (*Aporia crataegi*)

▶ ROOSTING IN THE RAIN

Most butterflies escape the worst of the rain by roosting under leaves, but some of them stay out in the open. With their wings tightly closed like this black-veined white, the rain just runs over their scales and drips off. The wings dry almost immediately when the sun comes out.

Focus on

Skippers are not closely related to other butterflies. Most are less than 2 inches across, with swept-back wings that make them highly agile. Skippers beat their wings rapidly and can change direction suddenly in mid-air, quite unlike other butterflies. The name skipper refers to this darting, dancing flight. More than 3,000 species exist worldwide, including about 40 in Europe and 300 or more in North America. Most skippers are brown or orange, but some tropical species, such as the Peruvian skipper, have brilliant colors.

SHAPES
The body of this rainforest butterfly (*Haemactis sanguinalis*) is typical of all skippers. It has a plump, hairy body that is more like a moth's than a butterfly's. The tips of their antennae are hooked, not clubbed like other butterflies.

CIGAR CATERPILLARS
Skipper caterpillars are shaped like smooth cigars. They have distinct necks and their heads are usually different in color from the rest of their bodies. They normally live in shelters made of leaves and spun silk.

Skippers

NIGHT-FLYING SKIPPER

This Peruvian skipper is not as drab and moth-like as many skippers but, like moths, it flies at night. It flies with a whirring sound produced by its wing beats. This is another feature skippers share with moths.

TRINIDAD SKIPPERS

Most skippers in Europe and North America are dull shades of brown and many resemble moths more than butterflies. However, many tropical species are more brightly colored, including this pair from Trinidad in the West Indies.

THISTLE FEEDER

The silver-spotted skipper haunts chalk hills and flies close to the ground. It likes to roost and feed on the flowers of low-growing thistles. Although it basks like the large skipper (*right*), it shuts its wings in when the sun is not out.

GOLDEN SKIPPERS

The large skipper, seen here on knapweed, is a member of a group called golden skippers. They bask in an unusual way, flattening their hindwings and tilting their forewings forward. Male golden skippers have scent scales in a black streak in the middle of their wings.

Migration

Some butterflies and moths live and die within a very small area, never moving far from their birthplace. However, a few species are regular migrants. They are able to travel astonishing distances in search of new plant growth or to escape cold or overpopulated areas. Some butterflies are truly worldwide migrants in a similar way to migratory birds. Every now and then, small swarms of North American butterflies turn up in Europe after crossing the Atlantic Ocean. Crimson-speckled moths have been spotted thousands of miles out over the southern Atlantic. Nevertheless, butterflies are unlike birds in that most only migrate one way and do not return to their original homes.

Canada
Atlantic Ocean
Pacific Ocean
United States
Mexico
Central America
Migration path

▲ **MONARCH ROUTES**
Monarch butterflies (*Danaus plexippus*) migrate mainly between North and Central America. A few have crossed the Atlantic and settled on islands near Africa and Portugal. Others have flown all the way to Ireland.

▲ **MONARCH MASSES**
Every autumn huge numbers of monarchs leave eastern and western North America and fly south. They spend the winter in Florida, California and Mexico on the same trees settled by their grandparents the previous year.

▲ **KING OF MIGRANTS**
In March, monarch butterflies journey over 1,800 miles northward, lay their eggs on the way and die. When the eggs hatch, the cycle begins again. The month-old butterflies either continue north or return south, depending on the season.

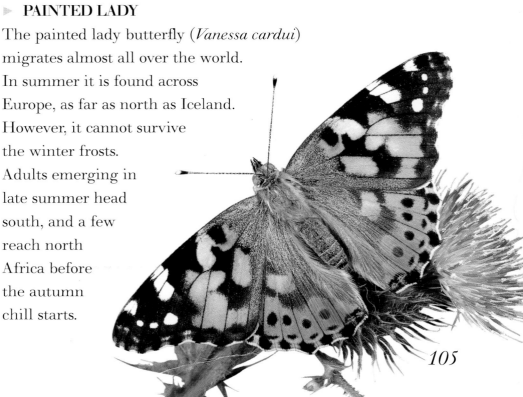

◄ AN AFRICAN MIGRANT

This brown-veined white butterfly has large wings capable of carrying it over long distances. Millions of these butterflies form swarms in many parts of southern Africa. A swarm can cause chaos to people attempting to drive through it. Although this butterfly flies throughout the year, these swarms are seen most often in December and January.

Did you know? A large swarm of migrating butterflies can bring farm machines to a standstill by resting on them.

► HAWK MOTH

Every spring thousands of Oleander hawk moths set off from their native Africa and head north. A few of them reach the far north of Europe in late summer. Hawk moths are among the furthest flying of all moths. They are able to travel rapidly over long distances.

Oleander
hawk moth
(Daphnis nerii)

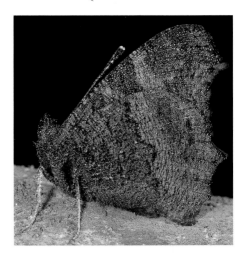

▲ HIBERNATING PEACOCK

The adult peacock butterfly sleeps during the winter. This sleep is called hibernation. The peacock is protected by chemicals called glycols that stop its body fluids from freezing. Many other butterflies and moths survive the winter in this way instead of migrating.

► PAINTED LADY

The painted lady butterfly (*Vanessa cardui*) migrates almost all over the world. In summer it is found across Europe, as far as north as Iceland. However, it cannot survive the winter frosts. Adults emerging in late summer head south, and a few reach north Africa before the autumn chill starts.

105

Enemies and Disease

Many butterflies and moths lay huge numbers of eggs. Sometimes a single female can lay more than a thousand at any one time. However, these eggs are attacked by predators, parasites and diseases from the moment they are laid. Caterpillars and adults also have many enemies and are preyed on by creatures such as birds, bats, lizards, spiders, hornets, and beetles. They are also attacked by parasitic wasps and flies that lay eggs inside caterpillars' bodies. Those that survive the attacks of these predators and parasites may fall victim to diseases or harmful fungi.

▲ **DEADLY BIRDS**

Birds are the most dangerous enemies of butterflies and moths. Many types of bird prey upon adult insects. In spring, birds such as blue jays are often seen flying back to their nests with beakfuls of fat, juicy caterpillars for their young.

▲ **BAT ATTACK**

An eyed hawk moth is devoured by a serotine bat, leaving only its wings and eggs. Night-flying moths often fall victim to bats, who can track them down in pitch darkness.

▲ **PROWLING FOXES**

Foxes would seem to be unlikely predators of caterpillars. Surprisingly, though, when scientists have examined the stomach contents of dead foxes, they have found huge amounts of caterpillars. Foxes are sometimes forced to eat caterpillars when other food is scarce.

▶ UNWELCOME GUESTS

An eyed hawk moth caterpillar is killed by parasitic flies of the Tachinidae family. Many caterpillars are killed in this way. The fly injects its eggs into the caterpillar's body, and the newly hatched grubs eat away the body from the inside. The grubs grow and eventually bore their way out.

Gatekeeper butterfly
(*Pyronia tithonus*)

clump of red mites

◀ RED MITES

The red blob on the back of this gatekeeper butterfly is a clump of red mites. These mites are larvae that cling to butterflies of the Satyridae family. They feed on the butterfly's blood until they are full, and then drop off, apparently doing the butterfly little harm.

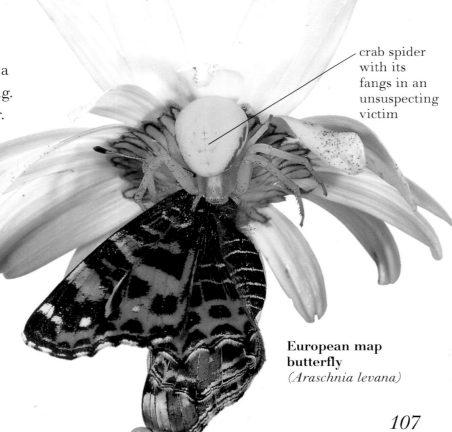

crab spider with its fangs in an unsuspecting victim

▶ POUNCING SPIDERS

A butterfly that is sitting motionless on a flower for a long time may not be resting. It may have been killed by a crab spider. Creamy-yellow crab spiders blend in so well on flower heads that many butterflies do not notice them and fall victim to their deadly venom.

Did you know? Chinese herbal medicine uses ground-up caterpillars from which fungi have grown.

European map butterfly
(*Araschnia levana*)

107

Camouflage

Citrus swallowtail butterfly pupa *(Papilio demodocus)*

◄ **PUPA PROTECTION**
A citrus swallowtail butterfly pupa mimics a curled-up green leaf. Pupae remain motionless for weeks and are highly vulnerable, so camouflage is often their only protection.

Caterpillars and adult butterflies and moths are so vulnerable to attack that many have become masters of disguise. They hide from prying eyes by taking on the colors of trees, leaves and rocks. This defense is known as camouflage. Many moths fold back their wings during the day so they look like leaves or a pieces of bark. Most caterpillars are green to mimic leaves and grass or brown to mimic bark and mud. Inchworms (the caterpillars of looper moths) are colored and shaped to look just like twigs and even cling to stems at a twiglike angle.

Did you know? Emperor moth caterpillars blend in with heather leaves when small and heather stems when they grow larger.

▼ **LEAF MIMIC**
A wing of the Brazilian butterfly *Zaretis itis* looks like a dead leaf. The wing even mimics a leaf's natural tears and the spots made on it by fungi.

▲ **LYING LOW**
Geometrid moths are not easy to spot among dead leaves on the floor of a rainforest in Costa Rica. Another Costa Rican moth disguises itself as lichen. Moths rest in broad daylight, so they need to be especially well camouflaged.

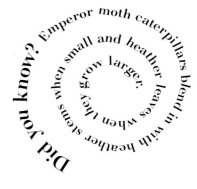

Zaretis itis

▲ HIDDEN LARVA

The caterpillar of the orchard swallowtail butterfly is camouflaged as a bird-dropping. Other caterpillars are brown or green, so they blend in with vegetation.

▲ FOLIAGE FRIENDLY

A brimstone butterfly camouflages itself as a leaf by folding up its wings so that only the green underside is visible. The upper side of this butterfly's wings is the color of brimstone (bright yellow), which is how the insect got its name.

Did you know? The moth Belenoptera sanguine rests with the front of its wings rolled up to resemble a leaf stalk.

▲ PINE MIMIC

The pine hawk moth *(Hyloicus pinastri)* is perfectly adapted to the pine forests in which it lives. Its mottled silvery-gray wings match the bark of pine trees. The moth is almost impossible to spot when it roosts during the day. Other moths imitate the bark of different trees.

▶ TWIGS

The peppered moth caterpillar resembles a twig. It even has warts on its body like the buds on a twig. In the 1800s, a darker form of the adult moth became more common. This was because the soot from factories made tree trunks sooty. The darker moth blended in better on the dark trunks.

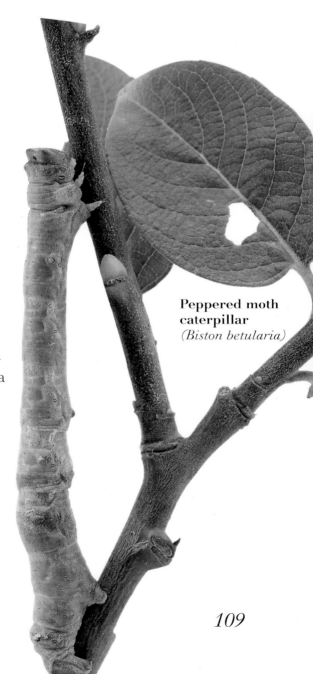

Peppered moth caterpillar
(Biston betularia)

109

Spotted tiger moth
(*Rhypasia purpurava*)

Decoys and Displays

Camouflage helps keep resting moths and butterflies hidden from the eyes of predators, but as soon as they move they become visible. Therefore, butterflies and moths that fly during daylight hours must adopt other strategies to escape. The upper wings of many butterflies are colored in all kinds of surprising ways to fool predators. Some mimic dangerous creatures. For example, the striped body, transparent wings and buzzing flight of a hornet clearwing moth make it resemble a stinging hornet from a distance. Others use colors or their wing shapes to confuse their predators. False antennae and eyes fool them into attacking from the wrong direction.

▲ CONFUSION

A spotted tiger moth escapes predators by surprising them with a quick flash of its brightly colored underwings. When the moth is resting, these wings are hidden beneath its yellow forewings. A sudden flash of color is often enough to confuse an enemy.

▶ BIG EYES

A Japanese owl moth (*Brahmaea japonica*) flashes giant spots at a foe when threatened. These spots look like the staring eyes of a big owl, which scares off birds, lizards and other predators. Other moths display bright parts of their wings while in flight. When they are being chased, the predator focuses on the moth's bright wings. However, as soon as the moth lands, the color is hidden and the predator is confused.

TRICK OF THE EYE

Eyed hawk moths have big eye spots on their hindwings. When in danger, the moth startles its enemy by flinging its wings open to reveal the enormous false eyes beneath.

eye spots are hidden by forewings

▶ SHUT EYES

A mating pair of eyed hawk moths hide their eye spots beneath their forewings. The effectiveness of eye spots depends on flashing them suddenly. To an inquisitive predator, it looks just like a cat or an owl opening its eyes—and the predator is frightened away.

Did you know? Some moth pupae produce squeaks to deter predators from eating them.

▶ TWO HEADS ARE BETTER THAN ONE

This Blue butterfly's secret escape system is the false eyes and mock antennae on its rear end. Predatory birds are fooled into lunging for the flimsy false head rather than the butterfly's real head at the other end. The butterfly then slips away from the bird's beak.

false eyes and antennae

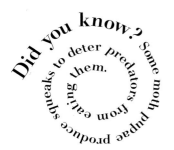

WASP IMPERSONATOR

The hornet clearwing moth loses most of the scales from its wings on its first flight and then looks just like a wasp. Birds fear that it has a vicious sting, although it is harmless.

▼ DECOY EYES

A little wood satyr butterfly has false eyes at the edges of its wings. A huge number of butterflies and moths have similar spots on their wings. Birds peck at them, thinking they are real eyes.

Butterflies are often seen flying with pieces bitten out of their wing edges. They do not seem to be troubled by having parts of their wings missing and are able to fly as normal.

Chemical Weapons

African Euchromia moth
(*Euchromia lethe*)

Most butterflies and moths escape their enemies by avoiding being spotted. However, some use other tricks. They cannot sting or bite like bees or wasps, but many caterpillars have different ways of using toxic chemicals to poison their attackers, or at least make themselves unpleasant to taste or smell. For example, the caterpillar of the Brown-tail moth has barbed hairs tipped with a poison that can cause a severe skin rash even in humans. A cinnabar moth cannot poison a predator, but it tastes foul if eaten. Usually, caterpillars that are unpalatable to predators are brightly colored to let potential attackers know that they should be avoided.

▲ BRIGHT AND DEADLY

The brilliant colors of the African Euchromia moth warn any would-be predators that it is poisonous. It also has an awful smell. Some moths manufacture their own poisons, but others are toxic because as caterpillars, they eat poisonous plants. The poisons do not hurt the insects, but make them harmful to their enemies.

▲ HAIRY MOUTHFUL

The caterpillar of the sycamore moth (*Apatele aceris*) is bright yellow. It is poisonous like some other brightly colored caterpillars, but its masses of long, hairy tufts make it distinctly unpleasant to eat.

▼ THREATENING DISPLAY

The caterpillar of the puss moth may look as brightly colored as a clown, but by caterpillar standards it is quite fearsome. When threatened, its slender whip-like tails are thrust forward and it may squirt a jet of harmful formic acid from a gland near its mouth. It also uses red markings and false eye spots on its head to create an aggressive display.

whip-like tail to threaten predators

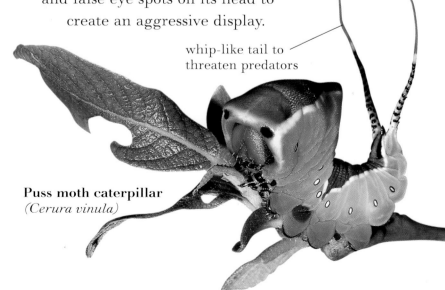

Puss moth caterpillar
(*Cerura vinula*)

POISON MILK

A monarch butterfly caterpillar feeds on various kinds of milkweed that contain a powerful poison. This chemical is harmful to many small creatures. The poison stays in the monarch's body throughout its life. This may be why monarchs show less fear of predators than other butterflies.

RED ALERT

The striking red, white and black colors of the spurge hawk moth caterpillar announce that it is poisonous. Unpalatable insects frequently display conspicuous colors such as red, yellow, black and white. These insects do not need to protect themselves by blending into their background. This caterpillar acquires its poison from a plant called spurge.

Spurge hawk moth caterpillar
(Hyles euphorbiae)

Did you know? Many harmless butterflies mimic poisonous species so well that enemies dare not touch them.

SMELLY CATERPILLARS

The swallowtail butterfly caterpillar produces an odor that is strong enough to ward off parasites. It comes from a scent-gland called the osmeterium situated just behind its head. This gland suddenly erupts and oozes acid when the caterpillar is threatened.

DEFENSIVE FROTH

Rhodogastria moths of Australasia often have bright red abdomens to warn others that they carry deadly poisons. When the moth is threatened, this poison oozes as a green froth from a gland on the back of its neck.

Swallowtail butterfly caterpillar
(Papilio machaon)

Around the World

Butterflies and moths are surprisingly adaptable creatures. Almost every land mass in the world has its own particular range of butterfly and moth species. They inhabit a great number of different places, from the fringes of the hottest deserts to the icy lands of the Arctic. Species are adapted to living in these very different environments. For example, butterflies and moths that live in cold areas tend to be darker than those that live in warm regions. This is because they need to be warm in order to fly, and dark colors absorb sunlight more easily. In mountainous areas, the local species usually fly close to the ground. Flying any higher than this would create a risk of being blown away by the strong winds.

Orange-tip butterfly
(Anthocharis cardamines)

◀ MEADOWS AND WAYSIDES

Farmland is an increasingly hostile habitat for butterflies. Intensive cultivation strips away wild flowers and grasses, while crop-spraying poisons the insects. However, many butterflies still thrive in meadows and hedgerows around the fields. Orange-tips, meadow browns, gatekeepers, small coppers, whites and blues are still common, as are noctuid and geometrid moths.

Apollo butterfly
(Parnassius apollo)

◀ MOUNTAINS

Butterflies that are adapted to life high on the mountains include the alpine and mountain arguses and the Apollo. The Apollo's body is covered with fur to protect it from the extreme cold. Most Apollo eggs that are laid in autumn do not hatch until the following spring because of the low temperatures. Those caterpillars that do hatch hibernate immediately.

◀ MARSHES AND WETLANDS

The marsh fritillary butterfly flourishes among the grasses and flowers of wetlands in temperate regions (areas that have warm summers and cold winters). Its caterpillar's favorite food plant is devil's bit scabious. Among the other butterflies that thrive in wetlands are the swallowtail, the white peacock and the painted skipper.

DIFFERENT HABITATS

Butterflies and moths inhabit a wide range of regions. Butterfly species such as the large white live inland, while Spanish festoons, graylings and Two-tailed pashas often live in coastal areas. Deserts are home to painted ladies, while white admiral butterflies flutter around in woodland glades, as do pine hawk moths and lappet moths. Arctic species include the pale Arctic clouded yellow butterfly and Apollos are examples of alpine types.

GARDENS

All kinds of butterflies and moths visit gardens, including the peacock butterfly (*Inachis io*). Here they find an abundance of flowers to feed on—not only weeds, but also many garden flowers. Many of these flowers are actually related to wild hedgerow and field flowers such as buddleias, aubretias and Michaelmas daisies.

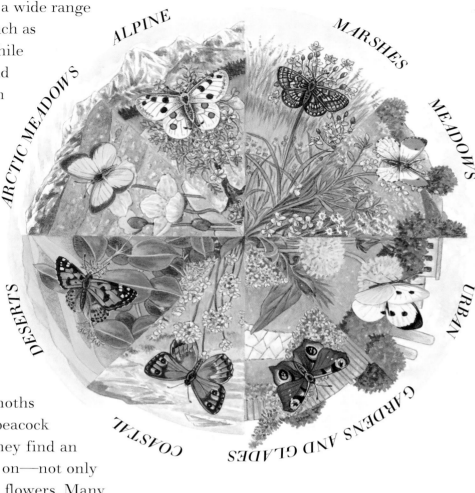

The Warrior Symbol

A statue of a proud warrior stands at the ancient Toltec capital city of Tula in Mexico. An image of a butterfly appears on the warrior's breastplate. The Toltec people knew that butterflies live short but brilliant lives. Consequently, the butterfly became a symbol for Toltec soldiers who lived brave lives and did not fear death.

Indian moon moth
(Actias selene)

Tropical Species

More species of butterflies and moths live in tropical parts of the world (regions near the Equator) than anywhere else. Tens of thousands of known species populate the tropical rainforests, and new species are being discovered almost every day. Some of the most spectacular and beautiful of all butterflies live in the tropics. These include shimmering blue morphos, vivid orange albatrosses and exquisite banded king shoemakers. A large number of striking moths live in these areas, too, including the Indian and African moon and the golden emperor.

▲ MOONLIT MOTH

The ghostly green-white wings of the moon moth shine dimly on moonlit nights in forests ranging from Indonesia to India. Its huge wings measure about 5 inches in width and up to 7 inches in length. The long tails, which are shaped like crescent moons, flutter in the shadows beneath the trees.

Painted lady butterfly
(Vanessa cardui)

▲ POSTMAN BUTTERFLY

The brightly colored postman butterfly is found throughout much of South America and has many different subspecies. These butterflies eat pollen as well as nectar.

▲ DESERT WANDERER

The painted lady butterfly lives in warm regions, although in summer it is often seen far to the north in Europe and North America. In autumn, it flies south to avoid perishing in the cold. In Africa, the natural homes of this species are the edges of the Sahara desert.

116

EMERALD JEWEL

The swallowtail family of butterflies (known by scientists as the Papilionids) includes some of the biggest and most beautiful of all butterflies. Among the most prized is the shimmering green *Papilio palinurus* that lives in the rainforests of Southeast Asia. Its green coloring blends in perfectly with the lush vegetation. Many types of swallowtail are protected species because of humans cutting down large areas of rainforest.

Green swallowtail butterfly
(Papilio palinurus)

METALMARK

A metalmark butterfly (*Caria mantinea*) feeds on salts from damp ground. This butterfly is one of the metalmark (or Riodinidae) family. It is one of the few families that are almost entirely restricted to the tropics. Their distinctive, rapid zigzag flight is often seen in rainforests.

WISE OWL

Owl butterflies, such as *Caligo memnon* of South and Central America, are some of the most distinctive of all tropical butterflies. Their large eyespots suggest the staring eyes of owls. They feed mainly on bananas. For this reason, many owners of banana plantations regard these butterflies as pests.

Did you know? The cattle heart swallowtail butterfly of Central and South America flies at heights of up to 4,900 feet along the edges of rainforests.

Owl butterfly
(Caligo memnon)

Purple hairstreak butterfly
(Quercusia quercus)

Woodland Species

Butterflies and moths have suffered from intensive farming in open country, but they still flourish in woodlands. A small number live in dense woods where there are few flowers. Larger numbers gather around clearings or glades. Certain species live mostly at low, shady levels, while others prefer to dwell high among the treetops. The largest number of species live in mixed woodland, where food sources are varied. However, some species prefer particular kinds of woodland. For example, the pine hawk moth is common in coniferous forests, the lobster moth is found in beech woods and the green oak tortrix moth likes oak woodlands.

▲ OAK EATER

The purple hairstreak butterfly's favored food plant is the oak tree. It can be found almost anywhere where large oaks grow in Africa and Asia. The adults do not seek out flowers for nectar because they flutter high in trees to feed on honeydew (a sweet liquid secreted by aphids).

▲ SHIMMERING PURPLE

The lesser purple emperor (*Apatura ilia*) and its cousin the purple emperor are among the most magnificent of all woodland butterflies. Their rapid, soaring flight-style is highly distinctive, as are their shimmering purple wings. They can often be seen near streams and ponds around willows, where their caterpillars feed.

▲ DEAD LEAF MOTH

The Lappet moth is perfectly adapted to woodland life. When its wings are folded in rest it looks just like a dead leaf. Its caterpillar feeds on blackthorn, apple and other fruit trees, and is regarded as a pest by orchard owners.

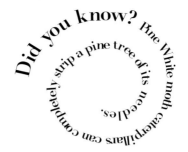
▶ FRITILLARY FLUTTER

The silver-washed fritillary is one of a large number of related butterfly species that inhabit woodlands. It can often be seen gliding through clearings and over woodland paths searching for nectar-rich blackerry blossoms. Its caterpillar feeds on violet leaves.

Silver-washed fritillary butterfly
(*Argynnis paphia*)

◀ OAK MOTH

The oak hooktip moth (*Drepana binaria*) lives in woodlands wherever there are oak trees. It flies mainly at night, but is sometimes seen on sunny afternoons. Its brown coloring blends perfectly with the bark on which it rests. Its caterpillar feeds on oak leaves. When it is fully grown, it pupates inside a cocoon spun between two oak leaves.

The Legend of Etain

An old Irish myth tells of Etain, who became a butterfly. At first, he was changed into a puddle by his first wife, who was jealous when he remarried. A worm was born from the puddle. This turned into a beautiful butterfly, which was sheltered and guarded by the gods.

▲ SPOTS AND STREAKS

The brindled beauty moth gets its name from the feathery bands on its wings. The word brindled means marked with spots or streaks. As well as living in woods, it is common in parks and gardens. Its caterpillar eats the leaves of various trees.

Focus on

Hawk moths are perhaps the most distinctive of all the moth families. Their scientific name is *Sphingidae*. Their bodies are unusually large and they are strong fliers. Hawk moths can fly at speeds of up to 31 miles an hour, and many hover like hummingbirds while feeding from flowers. Many hawk moths have very long tongues that enable them to sip nectar from even the deepest flowers. When these moths come to rest, their wings usually angle back like the wings of a plane. Hawk moth caterpillars nearly all have pointed horns on the end of their bodies.

1 Hawk moths begin life as eggs laid on the leaves of the food-plant. The round eggs are a distinctive shiny green. They are laid singly or in small batches and hatch a week or two afterward.

2 The elephant hawk moth's name comes from the ability of its caterpillar to stretch out its front segments like an elephant's trunk. It takes about six weeks to fully grow and, like most hawk moths, it passes the winter in the pupal stage.

3 The adult elephant hawk moth is one of the prettiest of all moths. It flies for a few weeks in the summer. Its candy-pink wings are a perfect match for the pink garden fuchsias and wild willow-herbs on which it lays its eggs.

Hawk Moths

POPLAR HAWK MOTHS

During the late spring and summer, Poplar hawk moths can often be seen flying toward lighted store windows in European towns at night. They have short tongues and do not feed. Unusually for hawk moths, when they are resting during the day, their hindwings are pushed in front of the forewings.

Poplar hawk moth
(*Laothoe populi*)

HONEY LOVER

The death's head hawk moth (*Acherontia atropos*) is named after the skull-like markings near the back of its head. Its proboscis is too short to sip nectar. Instead, it sometimes enters beehives and sucks honey from the combs.

MASTER OF DISGUISE

The broad-bordered bee hawk moth (*Hemaris fuciformis*) resembles a bumblebee. It has a fat, brown-and-yellow body and clear, glassy wings. This helps protect it from predators as it flies during the day.

121

Conservation

Ever-increasing numbers of butterfly and moth species are becoming rare or even endangered. Their homes are lost when forests are cut down, hedgerows pulled up, wetlands drained and fields sprayed with pesticides. All wild creatures have been endangered to some extent by human activity, but butterflies and moths have suffered more than most. The life of each species is dependent on a particular range of food plants. Any change in the habitat that damages food plants can threaten butterflies and moths. For example, the ploughing of natural grassland has significantly reduced the numbers of regal fritillary butterflies in North America, while tourism in mountain areas may kill off the Apollo butterfly.

◢ MORPHO JEWELRY

Millions of brilliant blue morpho butterflies are collected and made into jewelry. Only the brightly colored males are collected, leaving the less colorful females to lay their eggs.

▽ AT RISK

The false ringlet is probably Europe's most endangered butterfly. The drainage of its damp grassland habitats has led to its disappearance from all but a few areas.

False ringlet butterfly
(Coenonympha oedippus)

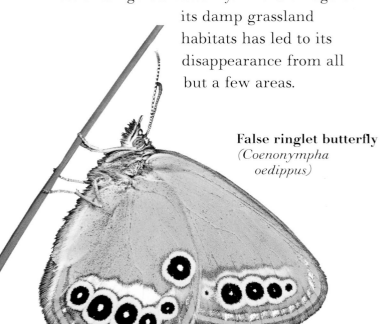

◢ FATAL COLLECTIONS?

In the 1800s, millions of butterflies were caught and killed by collectors. However, their activities had little effect on populations, because each adult female lays more than enough eggs to make up the difference. However, the destruction of their habitats in the 1900s has now made some species so rare that collecting even a few specimens may tip the balance against their survival.

Did you know? A butterfly collector once painted eyespots on the wings of a common species to pretend it was a new species.

PRIZED SWALLOWTAIL

The stunning scarlet swallowtail butterfly is found only in the Philippines. It is now under threat of extinction as its rainforest habitat is destroyed by urban development. Thoughtless collectors also trap this insect as a highly prized specimen.

SLASH AND BURN

Rainforests are burned down by developers to create new farmland and towns. Many species of butterfly and moth are threatened by the destruction of their habitats.

Scarlet swallowtail butterfly
(*Papilio rumanzovia*)

PUSHED OUT

The Kentish glory (*Endromis versicolora*) moth became extinct in England in the 1960s. This occured when the birchwoods in which it lived were destroyed.

ANCIENT MEXICO

The ancient civilizations of Mexico were fascinated by the many brilliant butterflies that inhabit this part of the world. The people of Teotihuacan (around 150 B.C.–A.D. 650) adorned some of their temples with butterfly carvings. The Aztecs (around A.D. 1200–1525) also worshipped a butterfly god.

GLOSSARY

abdomen
The abdomen is the rear section of an insect's body. It holds the digestive system and the sex organs.

adapt
When an animal, or group of animals, changes in order to survive in new conditions.

androconia
These are the special scales on a male butterfly's wings that release scent to attract females.

antenna
The plural of antenna is antennae. Antennae are the two "feelers" on top of an insect's head, which are used for smelling, touching and tasting. They are the insect's most important sense receptors. Not only do they smell food, but they hear and feel things, too. Some antennae may even pick up taste and changes in temperature.

basal region
The basal region is the part of a butterfly's wing that lies closest to its body.

camouflage
The colors and patterns on an animal's body that blend in with its surroundings, allowing it to hide from its enemies or creep up on its prey.

carnivore
An animal that feeds on the flesh of other animals.

carrion
Remains of a dead animal.

caterpillar
The second or "larval" stage in the life of a butterfly or moth, after it has hatched. A caterpillar has a long tube-like body with 13 segments and many legs. It has no wings.

cell
Any area of a butterfly's wing enclosed by veins — but especially the oval cell near the middle of the wing, which is called the discal cell.

chrysalis
The third or "pupal" stage of many butterflies' lives, when they transform into adults. They often do this inside hard, bean-shaped shells.

cocoon
A bag or shelter spun from silk thread by some caterpillars, especially those of moths, in which they pupate into an adult.

compound eye
The large eyes found on many insects, which are made up of many lenses.

cuticle
The tough substance that forms the outer skin of an insect.

diet
The range of food an animal eats.

discal cell
See cell.

ecdysis
When caterpillars molt (shed their skin) as they grow, the process is known as ecdysis.

elytra (singular: elytron)
The hardened wing cases of a beetle that have evolved from the insect's front wings. When the beetle is on the ground, the elytra fold over and protect its delicate back wings.

evolve
When a species of animal changes gradually over many generations to become better suited to the conditions in which it lives.

exoskeleton
The hard, outer casing of an insect, which acts as a skeleton and protects the soft parts inside. It is made of a tough substance called chitin.

extinct
When a whole species of animal has died out completely.

family
A scientific classification grouping together related animals or plants. Families are subdivided into genera.

fertile
An animal that is able to produce young after mating.

food plant
Any particular plant on which a caterpillar feeds.

fossil
The preserved remains of a plant or animal, usually found in rocks.

frenulum
The hook-like bristles that hold the forewing of a moth to its hindwing.

genus (plural: genera)
A scientific classification grouping together related animals or plants. Genera are subdivided into species.

gill
Part of an animal's body used for breathing underwater. Insects' gills are often feathery.

habitat
A type of place where certain animals and plants live, such as a tropical rainforest or a desert.

halteres
The balancing organs of flies. Halteres are the remnants of the hind wings and look like tiny drumsticks.

hibernation
A time when an insect is inactive or sleeping during the cold, winter months.

imago
The scientific name for the adult stage in the life of a moth or butterfly, when it has wings.

insect
One of a group of invertebrate animals (ones with no backbone). An insect has three body parts.

instar
A stage in the life of a butterfly or moth between any two molts or dramatic changes. The first instar is the newly hatched caterpillar. After its first molt, it enters the second instar. The final instar is the adult stage.

invertebrate
An animal without an internal skeleton. Insects, which have an exoskeleton, are invertebrates.

larva (plural: larvae)
The young of insects that undergo complete metamorphis, such as beetles, butterflies and true flies. Larvae can be grubs, caterpillars or maggots.

leaf litter
The top layer of a forest floor, consisting of dead and decomposing leaves.

leaf mining
Describes the way that small caterpillars eat tunnels through the insides of leaves.

lens
Part of an animal's eye, which helps it to see.

Lepidoptera
The scientific name for the group of insects made up of butterflies and moths. Lepidoptera comes from ancient Greek and means "scaly wings".

life cycle
Series of stages in the life of an insect as it grows up and becomes an adult.

mammal
A warm-blooded animal with a bony skeleton. Mammals feed their young on milk.

mandibles
The pair of strong mouthparts or jaws of a caterpillar.

mating
When a male and female animal come together to produce young.

maxillae
The pair of weaker, lower mouthparts or jaws of an insect.

membrane
A thin skin.

metamorphosis
The transformation of a young insect into an adult.

migration
The regular journeys made by butterflies and moths to follow seasonal changes in the weather.

minibeast
Insects and similar small animals such as spiders, wood lice, scorpions and centipedes.

molt
When a young, growing insect sheds its skin and grows a new, larger one.

nectar
The sweet juice made by flowers that provides the main food for adult butterflies and moths.

nocturnal
Describes an animal that rests by day and is active during the hours of darkness.

nymph
The young of insects that undergo incomplete metamorphis, such as bugs, grasshoppers and dragonflies.

order
A scientific category. Beetles and bugs are two orders of insects. Orders are subdivided into families.

ovipositor
The tube through which a female butterfly or moth pushes her eggs onto a leaf.

palps
Short stalks that project from the mouthparts of a butterfly or moth and act as sense detectors. They play an important part in finding food and food plants.

parasite
An animal that lives on, or in, another animal and obtains its food from it without killing it.

parthenogenesis
The process by which some female insects can reproduce without mating.

pheromone
A special chemical released by a butterfly or moth that stimulates another butterfly or moth – especially to mate.

predator
An animal that hunts and eats other animals for food.

proboscis
The long, thin tongue of a butterfly or moth. It is used to suck up nectar from flowers.

puddling
When a butterfly or moth drinks from a muddy pool or puddle.

pupa (plural: pupae)
The scientific name for the third major stage in the life of a butterfly, moth or beetle, before it becomes an adult.

pupation
The change from caterpillar to pupa or chrysalis.

retinaculum
The catch that holds the frenulum. It is used to hook together the forewing and hindwing of a moth.

roosting
Sleeping in a safe place.

rostrum
The long snout of a weevil.

scales
The small, thin plates that cover the wing of a butterfly or moth.

scavenger
An animal that feeds on rubbish and the remains of dead animals.

simple eyes
Small, bead-like eyes found on an insect's head that can detect light and dark.

social
Describes an animal that lives with others of its species in a cooperative group.

species
A particular type of animal or plant. The Goliath beetle is a species of beetle.

sphragis
The horny pouch that male Apollo butterflies ooze onto a female to prevent her from mating again.

spinneret
The organ of a caterpillar through which silk emerges.

spiracles
The holes in the sides of an insect's body through which air passes into breathing tubes.

stridulate
When an insect produces sound by rubbing parts of the body together.

succinct pupa
A pupa or chrysalis that is held pointing upward by a silkenthread.

suspended pupa
A pupa or chrysalis that is hanging down from a small pad of silk.

tarsi
The feet of a butterfly or moth. The tarsi often contain important taste organs.

territory
An area that an animal uses for feeding or breeding. Animals will defend their territory against others of their species

thorax
The middle section of an insect's body. The insect's wings and legs are attached to the thorax. The thorax is packed with strong muscles that move the wings and legs.

tympanal organs
The "ears" on the abdomen or thorax of an insect. The tympanal organs are made up of small holes, each one covered by a membrane.

veins
The thin, hollow tubes which support an insect's wings. The pattern of veins (venation) is often used to classify butterflies and moths.

warning colors
Distinctive colors, often combinations of red, yellow and black, which are common to many foul-tasting or poisonous animals, and which warn predators away.

INDEX

PICTURE CREDITS

b=bottom, t=top, c= centre, l= left, r= right

Heather Angel: 10tr, 81bl & r; Ardea London: /Steve Hopkin: 4t /M. Watson: 5b, P. Morris: 122tr; Art Archive: 13br, 45tl; BBC Natural History Unit: 4br, 26t, 61tl, 65; Bridgeman Art Library: 68cr (The legend of Cupid and psyche by Angelica Kauffman [1741-1807] Museo Civico Rivoltello), 119bl ("Etain, Helen, Maeve and Fand, Golden Deirdre's Tender Hand". Illustration from 'Queens' by J. M. Synge by Harry Clarke [1890-1931] Private collection); M. Chinery: 90tl, 95cl, 100tr, 103cl, 110tl, 111bl, 112tl, 122bl; Bruce Coleman: I. Arndt: 5tr, 104bl, 114c /J. Brackenbury: 99bl /B. Coleman: 118bl /G. Cubitt: 100cr /G. Dore: 114bl /P. Evans: 109bl, 115bl /M. Fogden: 80tl, 108bl /B. Glover: 97cl /Sir J. Grayson: 87tl /D. Green: 94bl /F. Labhardt: 74cr, 113tc /G. McCarthy: 72br, 103bl /L. Claudio Marigo: 108br, 122cr /A. Purcell: 72bl, 97tr, 107tr, 117br, 118br, 119cl /M. Read: 123tl /J. Shaw: 92tl /J. Taylor: 113tl /K. Taylor: 73cl, 85br, 87br, 91tl & cr, 114tr, 116br, 123bl /C. Varndell: 119tr /C. Wallace: 117tr, 123cr /W. C. Ward: 112br /R. Williams: 116bl; Mary Evans: 77cr, 87cl, 91cl, 95tl; Corbis: 49tl; Ronald Grant Archive: 9tr; Kobal Collection: 59tr; FLPA: R. Austing 104br /B. Borrell: 76bl /R. Chittenden: 111tl /C. Newton: 111tr /F. Pölking 98tr /I. Rose: 105cr /L. West: 76cl, 111br /R. Wilmshurst: 101cl; Garden/Wildlife Matters: M. Collins: 99br /J. Fowler: 84ct /C. Milkins: 116tl; Nature Photographers: Paul Sterry: 119br; NHPA: 10br, 11bl, 16c, 18t, 18bl, 19b, 20c, 23tr, 23bl, 24t, 25tl, 25br, 26b, 31t, 32c, 33b, 41b, 43tr, 46t, 47br, 54t, 55b, 56, 57tl, 57b, 62, 65br /S. Dalton: 96cr /D. Heuclin: 71cl; Oxford Scientific Films: 9tl, 9br, 11t, 13t, 13bl, 15c, 15br, 19t, 19c, 21, 22r, 23br, 25tr, 25bl, 26c, 27b, 28b, 29t, 29bl, 30b, 31c, 31b, 33t, 33c, 34t, 35, 39tl, 39br, 41c, 42c, 43tl, 45tr, 45b, 47t, 48t, 49tr, 50b, 51t, 52l, 53t, 55c, 57tr, 59b, 60b, 61tr, 63t, 63br, 64, 65bl; Papilio Photographic: 23tl, 54br, 59tl, 61br, 72tr, 94tr; Planet Earth /P. Harcourt Davies: 85tr /G. du Feu: 75bl, 83cl, 86br, 88tl /W. Harris: 71tr, 85cl /S. Hopkin: 81ct, 86bl /K. Jayaram: 73tl /B. Kennery: 87cr /A. Kerstitch: 97bc /D. Maitland 84br; Premaphotos Wildlife: K. Preston-Mafham: 68tr, 74cl, 80bl, 96bl, 99cr, 102tl & br, 103tr, 107cl; Kim Taylor: 8t, 9bl, 12br, 14, 16t, 17t, 17b, 18br, 20t, 22l, 27t, 28t, 30t, 41tr, 46b, 52r, 53t, 68bl, 69cr, 70bl, 73cr, 74tl & bc, 76br, 77cl, 82tl, 83tr & br, 85bc, 86tl, 90br, 95tr & bl, 101br, 107br, 120tl, bl & r; Visual Arts Library: Artephot, Roland: 115br; Volkswagen: 15bl; Warren Photographic: 8b, 12bl, 15t, 16b, 17c, 20b, 24b, 27c, 29tr, 30c, 32t, 32b, 34b, 36, 37, 38, 39tr, 39bl, 40, 41tl, 42t, 42b, 43c, 43b, 44, 47bl, 48b, 49b, 50t, 51c, 51b, 53b, 54bl, 60t, 61bl, 63bl, 65t /J. Burton: 70br, 80br, 85tl, 89tr & br, 96tl, 100cl, 106bl & r, 109tl, 110br, 118tl /K.Taylor: 69cb, 71cr & br, 73br, 75tc, 76tl & tr, 77cb, 82bl & br, 85tl, 88bl & r, 89tl, 90bl, 91tl & br, 92bl & r, 93tl, tr & cb, 95cr, 98bl & cr, 101tr, 103cr, 105tl, cl & br, 106tl, 108tl, 109br, 112bl, 113br.

Thank you to Worldwide Butterflies in Sherborne, Dorset for their help in creating this book.